HOW TO SELL ANYTHING ONLINE

ANAITA SARKAR

FOUNDER OF **HERO PACKAGING** AND **SELL ANYTHING ONLINE**

HOW TO SELL

ANYTHING

ONLINE

THE ULTIMATE **MARKETING PLAYBOOK** TO **GROW YOUR ONLINE BUSINESS**

WILEY

First published in 2024 by John Wiley & Sons Australia, Ltd
Level 4, 600 Bourke St, Melbourne, Victoria 3000, Australia

Typeset in Warnock Pro 11.5/15.5 pts

© John Wiley & Sons Australia, Ltd 2024

The moral rights of the author have been asserted

ISBN: 978-1-394-27081-1

A catalogue record for this book is available from the National Library of Australia

All rights reserved. Except as permitted under the *Australian Copyright Act 1968* (for example, a fair dealing for the purposes of study, research, criticism or review), no part of this book may be reproduced, stored in a retrieval system, communicated or transmitted in any form or by any means without prior written permission. All inquiries should be made to the publisher at the address above.

Cover design by Wiley

Cover image © andrewvect/Shutterstock

Printed and bound by CPI Group (UK) Ltd, Croydon, CR0 4YY

Disclaimer
The material in this publication is of the nature of general comment only, and does not represent professional advice. It is not intended to provide specific guidance for particular circumstances and it should not be relied on as the basis for any decision to take action or not take action on any matter which it covers. Readers should obtain professional advice where appropriate, before making any such decision. To the maximum extent permitted by law, the author and publisher disclaim all responsibility and liability to any person, arising directly or indirectly from any person taking or not taking action based on the information in this publication.

C9781394270811_150724

Contents

About the author

Anaita Sarkar is the co-founder and CEO of Hero Packaging, an author, a keynote speaker, a business advisor, and a guest lecturer at Macquarie University. She is also the founder of Sell Anything Online, a global marketing company.

At their dining table in 2018, Anaita and her husband co-founded Hero Packaging, which is now an award-winning sustainable packaging company for e-commerce retailers. What started as a solution for Anaita's previous business, where she was using enormous amounts of plastic to ship her products, is now a global company that has sold over 30 million compostable mailers to over 65000 businesses.

Anaita's passion is e-commerce and marketing, and she is recognised for her ability to break down complex marketing concepts into actionable and practical strategies that help businesses grow profitably. In 2020, she wrote a book on the marketing formula that she used to scale two successful e-commerce businesses. Leveraging TikTok as her main marketing tool, she was able to sell over 4000 copies of her book.

This success led to the birth of Sell Anything Online, a company that provides business mentorship to hundreds of business founders, from small startups to large national retailers. She continues to provide free marketing and business tips on TikTok and Instagram, where she has now amassed over 320 000 followers. She also works with global tech companies like Google, TikTok, HubSpot, Linktree, American Express and Adobe on their content marketing strategies.

She has received several accolades for her businesses, including the Amazing Women in e-commerce Award in 2023, the Retail Champion Award from Smart Company in 2022, and the Best B2B Retailer Award at the Online Retail Industry Awards in 2022. Her insights and achievements have also been featured in publications such as *Forbes*, Entrepreneur.com, SBS, Smart Company, *Business News Australia*, Channel 7, and Mamamia, marking her as a prominent figure in the e-commerce world.

She has delivered talks focused on small-business growth, digital marketing strategies and branding to thousands of business owners and marketing students. Notably, she was a speaker at the internationally acclaimed SXSW conference 2023, discussing the future of the creator economy, and at American Express's International Women's Day conference 2024.

Above all else, her biggest achievements are her three daughters: Olivia, Chloe and Grace.

Acknowledgements

To my husband, Vik, who understands what it means to be a great partner, who has spent countless nights staying up while I wrote this book and who backs every decision I make.

To my kids, Olivia, Chloe and Grace, who have never complained about me working on weekends, who brought me snacks while I wrote this book and who make me laugh every single day.

To my parents who have given me privileges they never had, who supported my decisions even when they were worried about the outcome, and who still call me twice a day to talk about life and business.

To Brittney Saunders, Flex Mami, Rachael Wilde, James Reu, Jess Ruhfus, Daniel Flynn and Mark Bouris: thank you for being so generous with your time and answers. This book would not be what it is without you.

How to use this book

This book can be read from start to finish in a linear order or it can be read in parts. It has been designed to be kept on your desk at all times so you can refer to it as needed, depending what your business needs are at the time. This could be to get brand awareness or website traffic, optimise website conversions or increase brand loyalty.

There are five parts to this book:

Part I: The 5 core pillars of business

To have a strong and profitable business, you must have a strong foundation. This foundation is made up of five core pillars that need to be established before growth.

Part II: Understanding the marketing funnel

Within each part of the funnel, I will teach you which marketing levers to pull to turn a new audience into a customer. Each part of the funnel also represents a different goal in your business:

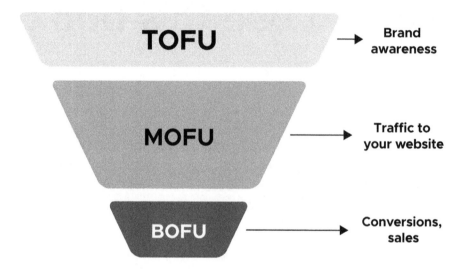

Part III: The secret sauce

The secret sauce is how to deliver an exceptional customer experience to existing customers and create raving fans of your brand. This section will truly set you apart from your competition.

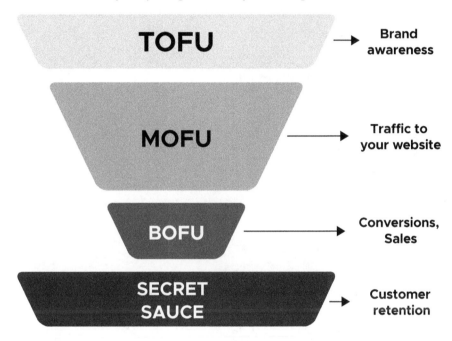

Part IV: The magic bucket

Creating loyal customers in your business is one of the cheapest ways to earn recurring revenue and build a community of raving fans. This section will show you strategies to convert one-off customers into brand advocates and fill your magic bucket with loyal customers, raving fans and brand advocates.

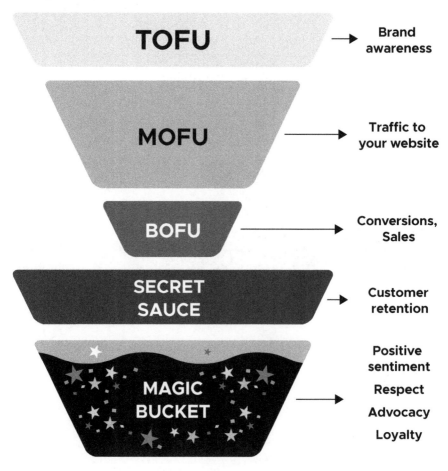

Part V: What's next?

This last section ties it all together, along with advice from Australian entrepreneur and business expert Mark Bouris, as well as information on how to build your community.

***

This book also includes valuable Q&As throughout and case studies from some of Australia's best brand owners and marketers. These will provide inspiration as well as a closer look at the ways they have achieved success in certain marketing areas.

Let's get started.

Introduction

'Do you know how to do anything right?'

Those were the words my manager yelled at me when I was working at one of Australia's top four accounting firms. It was 10am on a Tuesday morning. My manager had asked me to get a client file from the file room and I had mistakenly brought the wrong one. I remember handing it to him over the cubicle wall and within seconds he turned to me and said, 'This is the wrong fucking file. How hard is it to listen to my instructions? Do you know how to do anything right?' He dropped the file on the floor and turned back to his laptop. I was so embarrassed, not only because I had brought the wrong file, but because most of the people on level 12 now knew I had messed up.

I picked up the file and replied, 'Sorry, I'll get the right one.' I walked to the bathroom, sat on a toilet and cried. It wasn't the first time a manager had been rude, but it was the first time I had questioned why I was even there. I kept saying to myself, 'Surely this can't be my life.' After a few minutes, I heard the bathroom door open and one of my colleagues walked in and saw me crying. The words she said to me in that moment changed my entire life.

She said, 'You don't deserve this. I'm taking you to HR and you are going to resign. You're made for better things.' And that's exactly what I did.

After spending six years as an accountant at a company that made my parents incredibly proud, I resigned. But I was torn — I had spent my life working hard at school and university so that I could get a great job and eventually become a partner. That was always the plan.

But I was miserable, and I had been for six years.

After I left my job, I had no idea what I was going to do, but I knew what I didn't want. I didn't want to:

- feel like a tiny cog in a huge machine, and not understand what the machine actually did

- be yelled at for making a mistake

- work 12 hours a day and weekends for a minimal salary and no recognition.

To this day, those are my three driving forces in business. Even on my worst days, I remind myself of why I wanted to start.

And that's what I want you to do as the first activity in this book. Get a piece of paper and write down the three or four reasons why you started a business, and why you don't want to work for someone else. These are your driving forces. Take that page and put it somewhere you will see it every day.

There will inevitably be days when you question everything in your business, and in those times, there is no one who pushes you to keep going more than yourself. Always keep those driving forces in your line of sight. You're going to need them.

From employee to business owner

After resigning from my job, I tried my hand at a number of other jobs, from media buying for the Commonwealth Bank to marketing at a small telecommunications company. No matter how interesting the work was or how great the culture was, I was still miserable. So, much to the dismay of my parents, I quit each job within 12 months of starting.

According to them, I was lost.

What my parents didn't know was that I had started importing handbags from Alibaba (a wholesale marketplace) and was selling them on eBay in my spare time. I spent my nights learning how to create incredible product listings and I kept tweaking and perfecting them to get more visibility. Every time someone made a purchase, I felt so excited. While the sales weren't enough to replace a full-time income, selling products online made me incredibly happy. I didn't feel like a small cog — I was in charge of the whole machine.

After quitting my third job, I decided to not apply for another one. Instead, I decided to go all-in on starting a business. It was risky and unconventional and there was no guarantee of an income. So, I gave myself six months to achieve three goals:

◆ make $10 000

◆ receive at least one order every single day

◆ have customers make repeat purchases.

I told myself that if I could achieve these goals, I had the foundation for a strong business, and I would never have to get another job. I got to work very quickly.

These are the steps I took to start my business:

- *Found a product:* I looked for a trending product and found that personalised leather accessories, such as card holders and pouches, were in high demand. At the time, there were only two main competitors in the market.

- *Found a manufacturer:* After researching on Alibaba, I found a manufacturer selling leather cardholders. I ordered the minimum-order quantity, which was 100 pieces.

- *Found a personalisation tool:* In order to do the personalisation, I needed a tool to emboss people's initials on the leather. I found a handheld hot stamping tool on Etsy.

- *Created a business name:* I used my daughter's name as inspiration.

- *Set up a selling platform:* I had no idea how to set up a website, but I knew that marketplaces had millions of active users, so I set up an eBay store and an Etsy store. From my time selling imported handbags on eBay, I knew how to create a great product listing, so I used that knowledge to build both storefronts.

- *Worked out my competitive advantage:* I knew I couldn't compete with the two big competitors with their paid marketing or public relations, so I focused on the customer experience. I looked up the negative reviews of my competitors and saw that customers experienced slow dispatch times and terrible customer service, so I made sure I excelled in those.

- *Set my pricing:* I would not advise most businesses to compete on price, but I knew that if people were searching on eBay, they were searching for the lowest price, and so I priced my cardholders $10 cheaper than my competitors.

It took two months from idea generation to launching my business.

Within the first week of starting my business, I had sold ten personalised cardholders.

Within three weeks, I had my first repeat customer.

Within two months, I had to purchase the next batch of inventory from my manufacturer.

Within four months, I had made $10000.

I had hit my goals, but I also had a huge realisation. I was unbelievably happy. This was what I had always wanted to feel in my career. For years I had searched for a sense of pride in my work, but never found it. I realised that my satisfaction was never going to come from money or a job title, it came from having the freedom to try new things, test different strategies, talk to customers and control the business process from product generation to sale.

Starting a second business

Fast forward two years to 2018, I had a small office with three staff and three commercial monogramming machines, and we were shipping off 60 to 80 orders a day. One day, during the school holidays, we had packed all our orders and were waiting for the postal worker to come and collect all the packages, but as I looked around the room, all I could see was plastic. All the orders were packed inside single-use plastic mailers, and I knew that inside those mailers was plastic bubble wrap. I also saw my two daughters sitting on the ground playing with plastic bubble wrap and it made me feel pretty disgusted. I had never truly considered sustainability in my business before, but I knew that the amount of plastic I was using was terrible for the environment. When I got home that day, I was determined to find a replacement for those plastic mailers. I wanted something that looked like plastic but could be composted or dissolved. I searched online for days but came up empty-handed.

So, just like any entrepreneur, I said, 'I'll just create it myself!'

Over a period of nine months, I designed a prototype, sourced manufacturers, ordered samples, tested them in my home compost bin, re-designed it, ordered more samples, switched manufacturers, composted more samples, tested them for packing and shipping products, and finally came up with a compostable mailer that I loved.

I ordered 10 000 white compostable mailers to use in my business.

I was pretty chuffed with myself—I was eliminating single-use plastic in my small business, and I had created something that didn't already exist. I remember talking about the mailers on my Instagram stories and I asked if any other business owners would like to try them. Within 24 hours, I had dozens of people asking for a sample.

So, again, in true entrepreneurial fashion, I turned to my husband and said, 'I'm turning this into a business.'

He replied, 'Go for it.'

As this was going to require a big investment to get started, I needed to gauge demand for a product like this on a bigger scale. This is how I tested demand.

I set up a very basic landing page using MailChimp (an email marketing platform). On the landing page, it had an image of a compostable mailer, a title that said 'Need sustainable packaging for your business? Get a free sample of a compostable mailer', and a form for them to enter their name, email address and shipping address.

To drive people to that landing page, I created a Google ad and targeted anyone who was searching for 'sustainable packaging' or 'eco-friendly packaging.'

In one week, we had over 1000 sign-ups. This meant we needed to ship free mailers to 1000 addresses around Australia. It was an expensive task, but incredibly worth it because I had not only gauged demand of the product, but I also had my first 1000 email addresses.

It was time to start the business.

These are the steps I took to start (but this time, I was not starting from scratch, I was starting from experience):

- *Came up with a business name:* I wrote down all the words that reminded me of the planet or saving the planet and I kept coming back to a TV show I used to watch when I was a kid called *Captain Planet.* If you're not familiar with the show or its opening song, Captain Planet is the titular hero and the whole premise of the show is about reducing pollution to zero. I just knew that I had to call the business Hero as a hat tip to my favourite earth-saving TV show. I bought the domain name and set up all the social media handles.

- *Designed the mailers:* I knew that the mailers had to be aesthetically pleasing in order for business owners to use them, so I chose a matte black and a matte white. But I also knew that I wanted to add a colour that was trending, so I also created a millennial pink mailer. I added the brand name on the front so that our brand would be recognisable.

- *Set up the website:* I used Shopify to set up the website and created the home page and three simple product pages for the three different colours.

- *Used social media:* I made sure to be active on Instagram and Facebook, and used hashtags so that anyone interested in small business or sustainability could find my business.

- ◆ *Set up ads:* One of the key things I did was to start paid advertising straight away. I knew that I needed a lot of brand awareness to grow quickly, so I used Facebook ads and Google Ads to capture my target market.

Hero Packaging was able to grow quickly because of its fun and Instagrammable approach to packaging, and its ability to help business owners become more sustainable in their businesses without making huge changes.

I was able to apply the digital marketing strategies from my first business to Hero Packaging, and they worked. It made me realise that all businesses can use the same strategies to sell anything online — they just need to know which ones to use at the right time.

After running both businesses for a couple of years, as well as raising two kids (with another on the way), my husband and I knew that we needed to let something go. We decided to sell my first business, and after putting feelers out on LinkedIn and Instagram, we found a buyer.

We were now able to focus on scaling Hero Packaging even faster.

Now Hero Packaging has become Australia's go-to sustainable packaging company with over 65 000 business customers. It has won several business awards and has been featured in hundreds of articles online.

My seven business beliefs

In my ten years of business, I've developed a set of beliefs that I live by. They have been created, not only based on my experience, but also on the hundreds of businesses that I've analysed and mentored. Here are my top seven.

1. Be everywhere, all at once, at any given point in time, in the cheapest way possible

Wherever your target market is hanging out, I want you to be there. If they're scrolling through Instagram, your stories should be active. If they are in a Facebook group, they should see your brand name mentioned. If they are searching for an answer on Google, your brand should appear with the solution. If they are relaxing at home, you need to knock on their front door. Okay, I exaggerate, but I think you get it.

Start with the cheapest marketing levers, such as search engine optimisation (SEO) and organic content creation, and then amplify your visibility with paid marketing. I'll show you all the marketing levers you need so you can be everywhere.

2. There are no magic spells

There is no business success that cannot be explained. From Culture King's $600 million business valuation to The Oodie making $1 million in one day to Showpo scaling to a $100 million business, I can pinpoint the exact strategies that made them grow. There is no magic involved.

They each used a few key marketing strategies to scale, but their winning tactic was knowing which ones to use at the right time with the budget they had available.

There is nothing these brands did that isn't in this book.

3. Don't work for every sale

Rich people don't make money by working more hours. They place their money into wealth-generating investments that do the work for them.

Similarly, in business, you should not be relying on working more to get more sales. If you only rely on organic Instagram content to generate every sale, you will tire yourself out. Your business will not be scalable or sustainable.

You must have consistent paid advertising spend, SEO and email flows working in the background to make sure that any sales you make from the extra work you put in is a bonus.

4. Build relationships

For years, I thought that networking meant attending events and awkwardly finding people to talk to in the hopes of finding good business friends. I went to many such events early on, and always came away disappointed and frustrated. It was all small talk and no substance.

One day, I had a brand owner, Claire, reach out to me on Instagram. We had always spoken to each other via direct messages, and we always engaged with each other's social posts. Claire's message read, 'I've finally gone full time in my business, and I have time to meet up during the day. I would love to do coffee with you soon.'

I jumped at the chance to meet another business owner in person, so I agreed. The next week, we met at a cafe and spoke for hours about business and marketing and life. I told her some of the issues I was having, and she suggested some solutions. I did the same for her. It was the first time I felt like a friend understood my business.

We took a selfie and posted it to Instagram and, very quickly, another business owner reached out and said, 'I didn't realise you were in Sydney. I would love to have a coffee.'

I started to build relationships and a network of people who were aligned with me. We helped each other out and learnt from each other. Six years after that initial coffee date, we are all still friends. We share ideas, news, trends, problems and business advice. This is my network.

But my network doesn't stop there. Over the years, I've pushed myself to reach out to people who I want to build a relationship with — founders, experts, marketers and people in the e-commerce industry. And most of the time, it worked. It's not about asking them for a favour — it's simply connecting with people who align with you.

These incredible people have pushed me forward in my business and have even helped pull me out of some challenging situations. I want you to start figuring out who you want in your network and reach out to them.

5. Stop giving a fuck

We care too much about everything. We care too much about what our parents say and what our friends think. We care too much about how many likes we receive or how many people unsubscribed from our email campaigns. We care too much about what our audience thinks of our grey hairs when we talk to the camera. We care so much that it affects our behaviour and stifles our creativity.

When you realise that no one notices — let alone cares about — those things, you will be able to create and grow without the fear of judgement.

6. Have a brag book

You will achieve so much this year, but many of these achievements come and go and we forget what we did.

Keep a note on your phone called 'Brag Book' and document every single thing that you achieve this year. Take screenshots, copy and paste reviews, take photos and upload everything into your brag book.

At the end of the year, you can look back on it and feel proud. But the best part is you can use your brag book to gather talking points. Inevitably, you will be asked to be on a podcast, on a panel or answer a written Q&A about your business journey. This brag book will help you remember every winning strategy so you can provide valuable answers.

7. Be delusional

Lady Gaga once famously spoke about an ex who told her she would never succeed, and she replied: 'Someday, when we're not together, you won't be able to order a cup of coffee at the fucking deli without hearing or seeing me.'

That's how I want you to think about yourself. You are the best at what you do, and you will succeed. Any problems you face are solvable. Facing them and solving them will only make you a better business owner.

You have an iconic brand, you are an iconic founder and you are made to do iconic shit.

A business is easy to start, but difficult to grow

A friend of mine wanted to start a business selling cooling eye masks. She had already done the sampling process and ordered 300 units from her Alibaba manufacturer. I told her to spend two days setting up her Shopify store, taking photos of the product, creating a product page, creating her first email flows and planning out her social media posts. And that's exactly what she did.

She also planned a big launch of her product by booking a paid influencer with a large following, directed people from her personal social accounts to her new brand account, and hyped up the launch on TikTok. She spent weeks planning the launch and she did a fantastic job. In fact, on the day of the launch she sold 120 of the 300 units. Her friends, family, her TikTok audience and the influencer's audience opened their wallets and bought her eye masks.

The launch was a big success, especially for someone who had never had a business before. I spoke to her on the phone, and I remember the excitement in her voice. She even spoke to me about her next product idea: a warming eye mask.

The next day, the sales momentum slowed a little, but she still sold another 40 eye masks.

Two days after launch, do you know how many she sold? None.

The day after that? Also none.

In the two weeks after launch, she had sold three additional eye masks.

When I spoke to her again, I told her, 'You can't simply rely on a big launch to make consistent sales. You need a different marketing approach to constantly find a new audience and to make more sales.'

Many people want to start a business. Some of them try and think of a business idea for months or years, and when they finally have an idea, they spend another few months procrastinating about it, then another few months making the website and then more months planning the launch. They invest time and energy into the beginning stages and get excited at launch because they receive their first few orders.

But what they don't realise is that they've just completed one of the easiest things in business. The part that comes next — the consistent sales and subsequent growth — is incredibly difficult.

The reason for this is because business owners need to do everything in their business. From website creation to social media posting, to email marketing, to accounting, to product planning, to customer service, to multi-channel content creation — they usually have to do this with little or no help.

Business owners know they need to have a clear strategy in place to continuously bring in new customers as well as keep current customers happy. But there is also an overwhelming amount of information available online. It's confusing and exhausting to sift through it all and find what works.

A lot of business owners also see other brands 'blow up overnight' and get disheartened. They wonder how those other brands magically became successful.

What they don't realise is that there is no secret sauce, luck or magical fairy dust that grows a brand. In fact, there are a finite number of marketing strategies (or levers) that any brand has access to. The successful brands just know which marketing levers to use at the right time, and some know how to use each lever better than other brands.

This is exactly what this book will teach you. You will learn about the importance of the marketing funnel and its three main parts: top of funnel, middle of funnel and bottom of funnel. You will also learn that each part targets a specific group of people with key marketing strategies designed to push people from the top of the funnel to the bottom of the funnel. By the end of the book, you will know how to capture a new audience and turn them into a customer. But, the customer journey doesn't simply end there. This book has detailed and actionable tips on how to provide those customers with an incredible experience and, ultimately, create brand advocates and loyal fans.

While this book is about implementing marketing strategies, it actually serves a much bigger purpose — to give you more time to do the things you want! It will help you automate your marketing so that you can make consistent revenue without working for every single sale, and will give structure to your weeks so that you are able to work on your marketing with clear goals.

The ultimate goal of this book is to alleviate the stress of not knowing how to grow your business. You will not only be able to implement strategies for growth, but will also be able to simplify your workflow so you can feel excited about the brand you are building.

PART I

The 5 core pillars of business

Businesses come in all sorts of shapes and sizes, from their product or service offerings to their audience and their branding. However, every business must have a solid foundation in order to not only grow, but grow profitably.

There are five things in common that all businesses must have:

1. Competitive advantage

2. Cash

3. Protectable intellectual property (IP)

4. Digital assets

5. Consistency.

These are your core pillars because they strengthen the foundation of your entire business. The marketing strategies in this book will only work if you build your core pillars from now.

CHAPTER 1

Craft a distinct competitive advantage

There are rarely any products that consumers cannot buy from another business, and usually they have the same features/benefits and the same price. Even if you are the first to market with an incredible product, your lead can be lost within months. In fact, another business may even create a slightly better version of the product than yours. Having a good product is not enough to give you a competitive advantage.

When I ask business owners what their competitive advantage is, I'm met with these common responses:

- *My products actually work.*

- *When a customer tries my product for the first time, they fall in love with it.*

- *My products make people feel good.*

- *I use the best-quality ingredients.*

My response is always, 'But what if another brand creates the same product as you with the same materials or ingredients? Why would customers choose you over your competitors?'

Most of the time, they don't have an answer.

If you focus solely on your product's features and benefits, you open yourself up to the risk of duplication — another brand could introduce the exact same product at the exact same price. And when that happens, you will be compared purely on price. That is a position you don't want to be in.

Rather than focus on product, I want you to focus on brand uniqueness and recognisability. The idea is that, no matter who creates a product similar to yours, customers will always choose your brand. Brand uniqueness and recognisability are about making your brand easily identifiable by consumers. Much of the time, it has little to do with your product itself, and has more to do with your brand colours, slogans, personality, customer experience and founder.

Brand recognisability is a long-term strategy and cannot be easily taken away. It is your true competitive advantage.

Let's look at a few examples of this:

Peter Alexander: The sleepwear king

Many brands sell sleepwear, but no sleepwear brand has more recognisability than Peter Alexander. From the dog logo to the smell of its stores, buying from it is an experience.

Competitive advantage includes its:

- famous gift packaging

- brand colours and logo

- store experience.

Go-To Skincare: founder-driven following

Go-To Skincare is one of Australia's most loved brands because of its brand personality, which is a reflection of its founder, Zoë Foster Blake. While the skincare is good, there are many brands that sell similar formulations; however, the brand has retained a cult-like following for many years.

Competitive advantage includes its:

- founder

- witty and fun brand personality, which feeds into all aspects of their marketing

- famous peach branding

- product innovation, including the release of a kids' line, men's line and brand collaborations.

Hero Packaging: Making sustainability fun

Yes, I am including my own company in this list as, while it is a relatively small player in the world of e-commerce, it has become the go-to packaging store for over 65000 businesses within five years. While the products do have competitors, it has created a loyal fan base who keep returning.

Competitive advantage includes its:

◆ bright branding colours and fresh take on the boring packaging industry

◆ founder (me): I showcase my authority in the sustainability space through keynotes, panels and content marketing

◆ Instagrammable products, like an influencer-designed compostable mailer and millennial pink printers.

I want you to think about your business and assess your competitive advantage. Think about what you would like your competitive advantage to be. Write it down and brainstorm what steps you need to take to achieve it.

CHAPTER 2

Master your cashflow

About two years ago, I met with a high-growth ventures company for Hero Packaging. The goal of any high-growth ventures team is to help fast-growing companies get their finances in order to, ultimately, sell the business. I felt excited because Hero Packaging had been growing incredibly fast and I wanted to keep that momentum going. I opened up Zoom on my computer (Sydney was in lockdown at the time) and I met its head of finance and an account manager. After our introductions, the first question they asked was, 'What is your cash runway?'

I had absolutely no idea what the term 'cash runway' was and when I asked them to clarify, the head of finance said, 'If your business didn't make a single dollar from this point onwards, how long would the cash in your bank last to pay all your fixed costs?'

I remember getting a sinking feeling in my stomach. I asked back 'What should my cash runway be?' She replied, 'Ideally six months, but even two to three months is okay. We can work with that.'

Immediately I knew that something was wrong in my business. We had no excess cash at the time, let alone a cash runway of six months. We were operating day-to-day — money in, money out. And I thought that was normal, especially because we were growing with higher revenue.

That Zoom meeting was a huge wake-up call for me. It made me realise why I was so worried all the time, and why the business was in a never-ending cycle of getting loans, paying them off over months and then getting new loans.

I had a fast-growing business that was getting over 100 orders a day, but no excess cash to show for it. But I was determined to change that.

How it should work

When you start a business, you should ideally start with a lump sum of cash. This amount of money will obviously vary between businesses, but whatever money you do start with, it needs to be enough to pay for technology, business subscriptions, inventory and marketing.

The idea is that you need money to kickstart the engines of your business. Then, assuming you sell through your first batch of inventory fast enough, you will generate enough cash to start covering your operating expenses, marketing costs and to invest in your next batch of inventory. The cycle continues on and on even as your business grows. Your business will generate profits and continue to accumulate cash over time. Easy, right?

In reality, cashflow in your business will rarely work this way because of a few key factors:

- ◆ Your product margins may not be high enough.

- ◆ Your inventory payments are required too far in advance of you making sales on that inventory.

♦   The cost of acquiring new customers is higher than expected.

♦   Most importantly, you are not making cash a priority.

When I first started, I wish someone had given me a crash course on managing cash in my business. I was so focused on the marketing and sales in my businesses, and only realised later that cash management is far more important. I have some tips that have made my business life much easier. Based on these, we are going to start future proofing your business so that you can breathe easier every day.

Before we get started, it's super important you understand I am not providing financial advice. These are simply some tips I have found useful in my own experience, and in no way replaces sound financial advice from your accountant.

Set cash aside daily

One of the first things I want you to do is to start setting aside cash every day. When sales come in each day or week, set aside 10 per cent of that cash in a separate bank account and another 10 per cent in another account. The cash in the first account is the start of your cash runway. The cash in your second account will be used throughout the year to help pay your taxes. This is to make sure you won't be scrambling to pull together funds when you owe the government money, regardless of which country you're operating in. You should ask your accountant for more advice regarding the frequency of the tax payments you need to make and allocate funds accordingly. But I have found using a straight rule of 10 per cent of revenue to be very helpful.

Let's go through an example.

Let's say you make ten orders a day and receive $1500 in revenue. Without looking at the bills or any future inventory purchases, set aside $150 in one bank account (cash runway) and $150 in another account (future tax). If sales remain consistent, in 12 months, you will have $54750 in your cash runway account and $54750 in your tax account.

Put the cash into a high-interest bank account

My next tip is to not just have all of this cash sitting in your regular bank account. Instead, the accounts you use to set aside funds should be high-interest business bank accounts, ideally from another bank to keep the funds at arm's length. The interest you collect on this cash is compounding, which means it grows based on the growing cash amount.

> **Tip**
>
> Look for high-interest bank accounts that don't penalise you for withdrawing funds and don't have a monthly fee.

Let's continue on with our example. If you put $150 per day into a high-interest bank account that has a 4.5 per cent interest rate calculated monthly, you will have $56050 in your account in 12 months. You have made $1150 by doing nothing.

This sounds amazing, but what happens if the cash you have remaining after you've set aside the two lots of cash isn't enough to cover your bills and inventory purchases? Then we need to address the three elephants in the room:

ELEPHANT 1: LOW MARGINS

Three years after starting Hero Packaging, we realised that the cost of our products had increased over time and so had our freight costs, but we hadn't raised our prices. This resulted in lower margins and more financial stress.

We knew we had to raise prices but didn't know if our customers would get angry or even switch to our competitors. After weeks of deliberation, the decision was made to increase our prices by 10 per cent on products we offered that our competitors didn't.

On the day we switched over to new pricing, we sat in front of our laptops ready for angry customer emails. We also prepared ourselves for a low sales day.

But none of that happened. We didn't receive any customer complaints, nor did we decrease our average sales. It was business as usual.

So, my recommendation is to look at your product pricing every six months. Have you kept the same pricing for years? Are you one of the best priced in the market? Did you launch your business with cheap prices but now can't sustain them? It is probably time to increase your prices. A good cash balance starts with a good product margin.

WHAT IS A GOOD MARGIN?

First, let's work out your product margin. This is the formula to calculate the product margin of one product:

$$\frac{(\text{Retail price without tax} - \text{landed price of product})}{\text{Retail price without tax}} \times 100$$

Here is an example. Let's say your numbers are as follows:

Product retail price: $100 (including sales tax)

Sales tax: $10 (assuming the sales tax rate is 10 per cent)

Manufacturing cost of product: $15

Freight cost for that product: $12

Import fees for that product: $3

This what we call the *landed cost* of your product: the total amount you need to pay to manufacture a product and get it shipped to your country (including product cost; the freight cost, such as sea shipping or air freight; and any import fees).

In this example, your product margin would be:

$$\frac{((\$100 - \$10) - \$30)}{(\$100 - \$10)} \times 100 = 67\%$$

Your product margin = 67 per cent

This will give you a product margin percentage and I assess those percentages in this way:

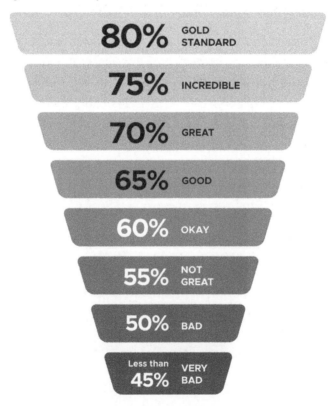

ELEPHANT 2: BAD SUPPLIER TERMS

The second elephant in the room is the payment terms you have with your suppliers. When you first start working with a supplier, the terms you get are usually pretty poor. It usually goes something like this:

- 30 per cent deposit

- 70 per cent once production has completed (and before the goods have been shipped).

These terms can really affect the cashflow of your business because 100 per cent of the inventory payment needs to be paid three to four weeks before the goods arrive at your warehouse/office.

If you have worked with a supplier once and you paid on time, you have the right to negotiate your payment terms. The next time you can negotiate terms something like this:

- 30 per cent deposit

- 40 per cent once production has completed (before goods have been shipped)

- 30 per cent once you receive the goods.

This is so much better for cashflow because you can start selling before the last 30 per cent is paid. In fact, you can even launch preorders and start making money before the last two payments need to be paid.

ELEPHANT 3: EXPENSIVE ADS

Your bills might feel too high because it is costing you a lot to get new customers. Perhaps you are running Meta or Google Ads, and the amount you're spending is not translating to sales.

What we are talking about is the cost per acquisition (CPA). This is how much it costs you to acquire every new customer. It is calculated by dividing the total cost of your ads by the number of people who have purchased from that ad.

For example, you might spend $300 on a Meta ad campaign and you received 15 purchases. Your CPA is $20. In other words, it costs you $20 to get each sale.

But how do you know if that is a good CPA?

A good CPA depends on your business, and more specifically, your average order value (AOV). If your AOV is $50, then your CPA should never exceed this amount. That means, it costs you, on average, $20 to acquire a customer and that customer will spend, on average, $50 in your store.

If your CPA is higher than your AOV, that ad is not working and should be optimised or removed. Remember, it is easy to buy revenue, but you can't buy cash in the bank.

CHAPTER 3

The power of protectable IP

In 2018, Davie Fogarty started The Oodie, a brand that is synonymous with late nights on the couch watching your favourite TV show. The Oodie is the world's first wearable blanket — a combination of a hoodie and a blanket. It is a product and brand that is loved by millions of people.

The Oodie has seen exponential growth in the last few years, and it all started with an innovative product. Davie himself thought of the patterns and prints on all the products and really leaned into meme culture. He used whatever was trending at the time to create new oodies.

But with every great product comes competitors. No matter how big or small a business is, if other people can see a product's success, there are bound to be copycats. It is an extremely frustrating situation to find yourself in. You have worked so hard to create something amazing, only for someone to come along and copy you. But, in most cases, it is inevitable.

Within a short amount of time, copycats of The Oodie started popping up everywhere — from small businesses to large retailers.

While this is extremely worrying for most brands, Davie knew that one way he could protect his brand was through licensing. In 2020, The Oodie did its first licensed deal with Warner Bros. They launched oodies with Harry Potter, Looney Tunes and Batman designs. Within a few weeks, he had made over $500 000 in sales.

At a time when he was worried about competitors, he changed his strategy and scaled. Since then, The Oodie has continued to licence many brands, including Disney, Nickelodeon, Pokemon and Barbie. By doing this, he has formed protectable IP (intellectual property) in his business.

This concept of protectable IP is critical. Business IP includes things like your brand, idea or creation. The problem is that many of those things can be copied. So, it's important for you to have protectable IP, which is the thing in your business that is unique to you, that no competitor can take.

When we started Hero Packaging, we were the first company in Australia to create home-compostable shipping mailers. Because we were first to market, had fun packaging colours and started using Google and Facebook ads quickly, we were able to grow quickly. However, we soon started to see many competitors enter the market. At first, we weren't worried because we had a lot of brand awareness; however, over time they started to copy our products (down to the exact measurements, thickness and artwork), our content from the website and even our ads.

In 2023, we knew that we needed to innovate our product, but also knew that anything we created would be copied. We had to find something that was difficult to do. So, we decided to introduce short-run custom packaging. We bought an expensive machine, we worked with a company to create water-based inks that were not toxic to the environment, and we spent six weeks learning how to custom print on our products. We are able to print on mailers, boxes and fabric bags with low minimum-order quantities. It was arduous and expensive to set up and launch, but this new addition increased sales significantly and has already generated hundreds of repeat orders. We created protectable IP for Hero Packaging that is hard to copy.

The more challenging and costly it is to bring something to market, the harder it generally is for competitors to follow suit. Having protectable IP in your business also increases the value of your business if ever you wish to sell the business or seek investment.

CHAPTER 4

Build your digital assets

Digital assets are groups of customer and audience data that your business 'owns'. These digital assets are critical to your business, and the more people you can funnel into these assets, the more value your business has.

Digital assets include:

- email subscribers
- SMS subscribers
- social media followers
- push notification subscribers
- Facebook group members
- mobile app users.

As a brand grows, these assets naturally get larger and larger. But I don't want you to simply let them grow naturally. I want you to focus on growing them through the marketing strategies that we will cover in this book. Once you have people in these assets, marketing to them is cheap and the return is high.

Some people argue that social media followers aren't digital assets because they are 'owned' by the social networks, but I disagree. If you have a group of people who have intentionally chosen to follow you because of your content or a recommendation, and you have a direct line of communication with them through direct messages (DMs), then they should be considered part of your digital assets.

Digital assets are the building blocks of any brand community because this is where you can directly communicate and converse with existing customers and people who are interested in your brand. These assets are fundamental to retaining customers, gaining customer loyalty and ultimately earning raving fans.

You must always look for ways to increase the size of your digital assets.

CHAPTER 5

Consistency will win the game

This is not a thing; it is a behaviour. But its importance is just as significant.

On Instagram, I did everything I could to grow. I posted more, I had other brands tag me, I had influencers mention me, I ran promotions, I did giveaways and I 'socialised' with other accounts. Do you know which of those tactics got me the most followers? It was posting more. I had been posting for a year until one of my videos took off. It got over 200000 views and 2000 followers within a couple of days. For an Instagram account of only 11000 followers, 2000 was a significant increase.

It took me a year of consistent posting to have one video to bring in followers and a tonne of people signing up for one-on-one calls. But I knew not to stop there. I kept up my consistent posting schedule regardless of how well a video performed.

What I see many people do is stop their consistent posting as soon as they get a viral video. They feel like they achieved what they needed to for a set amount of time, and they take a break. But that's a big mistake because that boost in brand awareness and sales is fleeting. Those things need continuation and persistence. See, the goal is not to do a task until you achieve something; it's to continue doing that task even after you have achieved that thing. You must stop focusing on the outcome (more followers, more likes, more sales) and start focusing on the process of doing one thing over and over and over again. That's where the magic happens. If you can do that, you will win.

The rule of 1000

In Gujarat in India (where I was born), there is a saying that goes, 'It takes 1000 days to be successful'. This applies to anything from business, to content, to fitness, to learning how to sew, to becoming more spiritual. Stick at something for 1000 days and don't think about the outcome. Think about being consistent and making progress every day for 1000 days or 1000 videos or 1000 sewing patterns or 1000 recipes.

Consistency will beat motivation every time.

PART II

Understanding the marketing funnel

A few months ago, as I was scrolling through Instagram, I saw a video ad for red exercise tights. I remember thinking how good they looked, but I kept scrolling. I didn't even look at the brand that was selling them.

The next day, I saw the same video ad come up in my feed. This time, I clicked through to the website, added my size to cart, and even made it to the checkout. Then I reminded myself that I don't need new tights (even though I really liked this colour). So, I left the website.

Lo and behold, within the hour I was seeing ads specifically focused on those red tights. I was also sent an email to remind me about my abandoned cart.

When I didn't give in, I got an email a few days later from the founder to talk about her brand and why she started her business. I clicked through to my cart and was very close to buying, but again stopped myself from checking out.

The final straw was when I saw someone who I follow online wearing green exercise tights from the same brand. She was doing a 10-kilometre run and talking about how much she loves the tights. It, too, was a paid promotion.

I immediately closed Instagram, went to Google and typed in the brand name. I clicked on the Google ad, had a quick look through the reviews and finally made the purchase.

It took seven days and eight touchpoints to make that purchase.

I had just stepped through a marketing funnel. All of the touchpoints I experienced between seeing the ad for the first time and buying the red tights were part of a planned, multi-channel effort to move me towards purchasing.

While marketers like to make it look complex and confusing, marketing funnels are actually incredibly basic in nature. I'm going to show you the marketing funnels and why they are so important for your business.

The marketing funnel is not a marketing strategy

In marketing, the 'funnel' is a concept that represents the various stages of the customer journey. It is not a marketing strategy. It's a way to categorise all the potential customers in your target market. We use the term 'funnel' because it helps visualise the number of people in each stage. Imagine, for example, that 1 million people have heard of your brand. Of those, 500 000 have considered buying. Of those, 250 000 are close to purchasing. Of those, 100 000 have purchased. Of those, 30 000 have left a review or repurchased, and of those 5000 are your loyal customers. These are the stages of the funnel.

It's your job to try and help as many people flow through the funnel as possible, all the way through to their first purchase and ultimately to brand loyalty.

The stages of the funnel

Let's look at the three stages of the funnel.

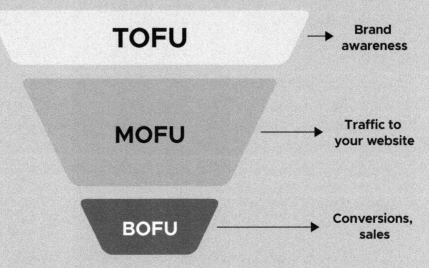

TOP OF FUNNEL (TOFU)

The TOFU represents people who have never heard about your business — we will call them a 'cold' audience. These people are your target market, but don't have any familiarity with your brand.

Type of audience: Cold

Level of familiarity with your brand: None

Your goal: Brand awareness

MIDDLE OF FUNNEL (MOFU)

The middle of the funnel represents people who have heard about your brand but have never purchased from you before. These people have either visited your website, engaged with you on social media or engaged with an ad. They are known as a 'warm' audience. Technically, they are easier to bring further into the funnel because they already know about you.

Type of audience: Warm

Level of familiarity with your brand: Medium

Your goal: Website traffic

BOTTOM OF FUNNEL (BOFU)

The bottom of the funnel represents people who are extremely close to purchasing from your business. They know your brand well, they've had multiple touchpoints with you and have added to cart. I like to call them a 'hot' audience. They should be the easiest and cheapest consumers to convert into a sale.

Type of audience: Hot

Level of familiarity with your brand: High

Your goal: Conversions/sales

***

The one thing in common between the people in each part of the funnel is that they are your target audience. The thing that separates them in the funnel is their behaviour.

At each part of the funnel, you need to implement different marketing strategies to target these people. We will go into detail for every stage of the marketing funnel and the ultimate aim — getting loyal customers into your magic bucket — as well as delve into the exact marketing strategies needed to push new audiences through the funnel to become loyal customers.

STAGE 1

Capturing your cold audience in the TOFU

Type of audience: Cold
Your goal: Brand awareness

You've probably seen certain brands blowing up seemingly overnight. Once you start noticing them, you see their brand name everywhere: social media, influencers, online articles.

You think to yourself, 'How did they get so popular so quickly?'

What you don't know is that you've probably seen their product and brand name many times before. You would have scrolled past an ad or seen someone using their products, but your brain hasn't retained their brand information. And now that you've noticed the brand and made an association between that brand and its products, you can't avoid seeing it.

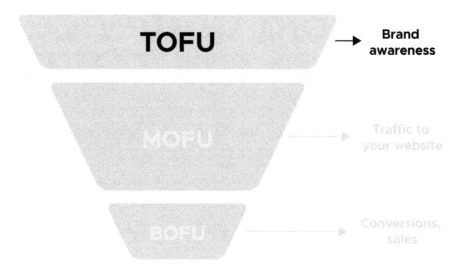

This is the effect of TOFU marketing. The idea of the TOFU stage is to show up wherever your target market is hanging out to ultimately get people to say, 'Oh, I know that brand', even if they've never purchased from you before.

Prior to the mobile phone era, creating mainstream brand awareness was one of the most utilised marketing strategies. Companies would pay for above-the-line marketing, such as TV ads, bus shelter ads, radio ads and even billboards, to get noticed by their target market. But the problem was that, at the time, companies were not able to effectively show their ad to their exact target market. They would run a television ad knowing that 70 to 80 per cent of the viewers were not their ideal target market, but the idea was to show up in as many places as possible to gain brand awareness, which leads to brand familiarity.

The same applies to brands today. While we have the ability to better target our audiences through strategic placements online, the broad idea remains the same: show up in as many places as possible so that people in your target market have some kind of familiarity with your brand.

If you can successfully generate brand familiarity for your business, you will have the best opportunity for people to flow through your funnel and translate into customers.

The subconscious power of brand familiarity

It is well documented that brand familiarity leads to brand trust. Brand familiarity occurs when a person sees your brand (and takes notice) multiple times. Many marketers say that a person needs to see your brand seven times before they will purchase, but I disagree. I believe that, on average, it takes at least 15 brand touchpoints before a consumer will even recognise the brand name, let alone purchase from it.

High brand familiarity can have several benefits for a company. It subconsciously enhances consumer confidence in the brand, as familiarity often breeds a sense of reliability and credibility, even if that consumer has never purchased from that brand.

It also affects a consumer's consideration set. A consideration set is a group of brands consumers compare and consider before making their final purchase decision. For example, if I realise I need a new T-shirt, my consideration set might include Uniqlo, Glassons, Cotton On and Kmart. Those are the brands I first think of for that specific need.

How did they become part of my consideration set? They have been actively visible to me over a number of years through physical retail, TikTok hauls, influencers I follow on Instagram and Meta ads.

But consideration sets aren't set in stone. In fact, new brands can enter consideration sets quite easily. Take, for example, my need for new activewear. For many years, my consideration set was Lululemon and Lorna Jane. But, recently, my consideration set has changed to LSKD and Stax.

How did this happen?

LSKD and Stax both have fantastic TOFU marketing. They show up everywhere I am online, and they now also have a physical presence. While Lululemon and Lorna Jane relied heavily on their physical stores to gain awareness, brands such as LSKD and Stax gained popularity through Meta ads and influencers. And it has worked.

There was one point when I had never purchased from LSKD, but I knew that during their sales, I would be buying their activewear over any other brand. That's the power of TOFU marketing.

CHAPTER 6

TOFU strategy #1: Facebook (Meta) ads

'Are you going to buy the BondiBoost brush?'

That was a question I was asked by my mum — the same mum who had never spoken to me about hairbrushes or any hair tools before. When I asked her where she had heard about it, she said she kept seeing the video of the brush on Facebook where 'the girl's hair was styled in five minutes!'

She bought it. And she bought one for me too.

My mum was a recipient of a very clever Facebook ads strategy created by BondiBoost.

BondiBoost is an Australian brand focused on professional hair care and, in 2021, they launched a new hair tool, The Blowout Brush. They had had enormous success selling their shampoos and conditioners and were trying to penetrate the hair tools category. Rather than focusing on only influencer marketing, which they had done for three years, they invested heavily in Facebook ads. They used the ads to get brand awareness to a new audience and targeted people in multiple age brackets and locations. When they went live with the new tool, they received over 20 000 orders, many of which were new customers, including my mum.

Their campaign was designed to reach as many new eyeballs as possible, and it worked.

Many business owners are wary of Meta ads (which we also refer to as Facebook ads in this book), and understandably so. They can be confusing and time-consuming. But, in my opinion, Meta ads are critical to gain brand awareness. It is always the strategy I start with when I speak to business owners, because getting Meta ads set up and firing allows you to get brand awareness quickly, even while you sleep.

Remember, people won't buy from you if they don't see you or remember you. This is the concept that I like to call 'brain space'. It is the amount of space a brand takes up in a consumer's mind, especially in purchase-making moments. As a brand, we need to focus on taking up more brain space, and we do this in two main ways: the first is by providing a great experience so that our brand is memorable and popping up wherever our target market is to prompt recognition, and the second is through Meta ads.

A common misconception of Meta ads is that they only drive conversions. While this is the ultimate goal, Meta ads can also help with brain space and brand awareness.

For the purposes of TOFU marketing, Meta ads are powerful because they can present a product to people who are likely to be interested in that product or category. They show those people the ad multiple times so that, eventually, they develop brand recognition.

There are multiple ways to run Meta ads to gain brand awareness. I'm going to show you how to set up two of my favourite evergreen brand-awareness campaigns: interest-based targeting and advantage plus campaigns. But, first, let's make sure you understand some of the foundational elements of Meta ads, such as the structure of the ad account, campaign objectives and budgets.

The structure of Meta ads

There are three sections or 'levels' of Meta ads. These levels are the campaign level, ad set level and ad level.

- ◆ Campaign level: This is the first level of the ad account, where you select the overall objective/goal of the campaign as well as the budget.

- ◆ Ad set level: This is the second level of the ad account, where you select the audience you want to target.

- ◆ Ad level: This is the third level of the ad account where you choose your ad creatives (your videos and images).

Campaign level: The objective

When you are creating any Meta ad campaign, most of the time you must set the objective of the campaign as 'conversions/sales'. Even though our aim is brand awareness, it is important to show the ad to people who are most likely to purchase from you.

If you choose another objective in your campaign, such as brand awareness or traffic, Meta will show your ad to as many people as possible, many of whom won't make a purchase. It shows your ad to the wrong people. This will spend your budget without getting you many returns in the form of actual website sales.

Campaign level: The budget

The amount you are willing to spend on Meta ads is based on many factors. Most importantly, you need to consider the revenue you generate per day, the average order value (AOV) for your website, your ideal cost per acquisition (CPA) and what you are comfortable with spending. See pages 13–14 for more on this.

However, there is a rule of thumb that I usually follow: test spending 10 per cent of your average daily revenue on Meta ads. So, if you make $500 per day in sales, your total ad spend on Meta should be $50 per day. This is for all campaigns in total.

However, if you're just starting a business, give yourself a monthly budget to spend on Meta. You may have allocated $5000 as an overall marketing budget to start your business. I would recommend you spend about $500 to $1000 per month on Meta ads.

Continue analysing your data to see if your website traffic and sales increase once you launch your campaigns. You can then adjust your campaign budgets up or down accordingly.

Now that we've covered the structure of the Meta ads account, let's move on to the two key campaign types you need to utilise to make sales.

Ad set level: Interest-based targeting

This campaign type allows you to specifically choose the demographics of your audience based on what they are interested in, what activities they do, what kind of job they have, what university they go to and their buying behaviours. It is a great way to broadly target your entire market. Let's run through an example of this type of campaign.

Business category: Kids activewear

Target market: Parents with kids aged one to seven

CAMPAIGN LEVEL

Objective: Conversions/sales

Budget: $20 per day (this is an indication only; refer to the budget section on the previous page on how to set your ideal budget)

AD SET LEVEL

This is where you choose your audience based on their demographics and interests.

The best strategy I have found is to keep the demographics as broad as possible. There is no need to narrow the audience based on age or gender unless you are certain that your product is only for a particular age range or gender. Meta already has a lot of data and will be able to serve the right demographic. Being too specific with your demographics may limit the number of potential customers you reach.

For the specific interests to target, here is how I would go about exploring these:

1. Start by typing in exactly who your target market is
    (e.g., parents).

2. Meta will give you a list of all parent-related interests.

3. Choose the interests that fit your target market (e.g., school parents, kindergarten parents and so on).

4. As mentioned already, I like to keep interest targeting more broad, but if you want to narrow it down, you can add an additional interest, such as 'exercise for kids'. Now you are targeting people who are parents *and* kids who enjoy exercise.

There is one additional step that you must do when creating your audience. You must exclude those people who have already visited your website or engaged with you on social media. Now you have a truly cold audience — people who are in your target market but have never heard of or interacted with your business. This ensures you're only spending money trying to obtain brand new customers.

AD LEVEL

This is where you will upload the videos and photos to build the ad creatives in your campaign.

When you are targeting a cold audience, it's best to be more direct in your messaging and visuals, rather than focus on storytelling. The goals here are to make people remember your brand name and build an association between your brand name and the products you sell.

AD LEVEL: TYPES OF AD CREATIVES

With Meta ads, there are different ad formats to choose from. You can choose from different ad styles, including:

- Image: One image in the feed

- Video: One video in the feed

- Carousel: A collection of two or more images or videos that can be swiped through

- Collection: One main video or image with some products from your catalogue appearing underneath.

Meta also allows you to view previews of your ad creative so you know exactly what it will look like to potential customers.

Creating the ad

Many business owners make the mistake of creating ads that are focused on the founder or include behind-the-scenes (BTS) content for their TOFU campaigns. These don't work well for two main reasons:

1. These audiences have never heard of you, your brand or your products before, so hearing a founder story will not make sense to them.

2. Because it's a new audience, their attention span is much shorter than if they have some familiarity with your brand. You don't have time to tell a story or do BTS content because they will simply scroll past the ad.

Here are some of the best-performing TOFU ads:

◆ Call-out image: A high-quality photo of your product with arrows pointing to different benefits of the product; for example, 'lasts for 12 hours', 'anti-smudge lipstick', 'comes in 18 different colours'.

◆ Short-form video: Product try-on with music and text overlay with one great feature; for example, 'Our viral leggings are back in stock'.

◆ 'As featured in' carousel: Lifestyle shots of your product with press or media mentions along with quotes.

◆ Short-form, TikTok-style video: Product explanation and features with a hook, such as 'If you have trouble sleeping, this silk pillowcase will change your life'.

Ad copy for TOFU campaigns

Your ad copy for your campaign includes all the text-based parts of the ad, including the primary text, headline and description.

Something that most people don't know is that you do not need to have a headline or description. Some brands, like LSKD, barely use these; however, I think it's important to have them because you should try and use every bit of real estate possible to engage your audience.

Let's break down each of the elements.

PRIMARY TEXT

The primary text is the first thing people read when they see your ad. It's the text at the top of the ad creative and is an important part of 'stopping the scroll'.

Here are some suggestions:

◆ use five-star emojis with a great customer review, such as '*****This eye cream cleared my dark circles in 5 days! I've been trying to get rid of them for years. I'm obsessed.' – Sandy G, NSW

◆ a question like 'Do you always get a headache in the afternoon? You need to try this'

◆ a bold statement, such as 'You won't believe what people have been saying about this blanket'

◆ a discount or sale, such as '40 per cent off this TikTok-viral journal'

◆ a quote from the press, such as 'One candle sold every minute!' – *The Daily Mail*

HEADLINE

The headline usually appears under the image or video, near the call-to-action (CTA) button. This is where you need to be clear, to the point and refrain from only using your brand name or having fluffy language like 'Try a beautiful product from our range', which has no marketing hook.

Ideally, a headline should include one of the following:

◆ what the product is; for example, 'The only beach towel you NEED' or 'The best creamy vanilla fragrance'

◆ puffery language like 'The best packaging in the world' or 'Try the jeans that went VIRAL on Instagram'

◆ a unique selling proposition (USP), such as 'Italian-made leather backpack'

◆ discount off first purchase; for example, '20 per cent off for first time customers!'

DESCRIPTION

The description is the small, un-bolded text near the headline and CTA button. This acts as the 'cherry on top' for your ad — it should add that last bit of excitement about the product.

Here are some examples:

◆ your extra edge, such as 'lifetime warranty'

◆ shipping information, like 'same-day shipping'

◆ order volume or customer data; for example, 'Over 1000 sold' or 'Join 20 000 happy customers'.

CALL TO ACTION

The call-to-action button makes it easy for your customers to directly access the products or services you're talking about. This can be as simple as a 'Shop now', 'Contact us' or 'Learn more'.

Advantage plus (ADV+) campaigns

ADV+ campaigns use AI to target people who Meta thinks is your target market. In this type of campaign, you do not need to choose your own audience as Meta will do this for you. So, unlike the interest-based campaign that we explored on page 34, an ADV+ campaign only has two sections:

1. Campaign level: Where you set your overall objective and budget.

2. Ad level: Where you set up your ad creatives. You can have the same ads as your interest-based campaign to test which campaign is best for TOFU, or you can have different ads with similar messaging.

Both of these sections are created in the same way as the interest-based campaigns.

Why do you need two TOFU Meta campaigns?

The reason you should have two TOFU campaigns is because you want to make sure that you create a very wide funnel opening to pull as many people in as possible. By targeting certain interests as well as allowing Meta to choose your audience, you are showing up in front of a big chunk of your target market.

Nice! You now have two top-of-funnel campaigns set up. Your goal of building brand awareness is off to a good start.

> **Tip**
>
> My top tools for Facebook ads are Facebook Ads Library and Foreplay. The Ads Library allows you to view any ads being run by any advertiser, including your competitors. Once you have a larger Meta ads account, Foreplay makes it easier to manage your ad creation process.

CHAPTER 7

TOFU strategy #2: Influencer marketing

I know exactly what you're thinking. Influencer marketing doesn't work anymore — you've either tried it with no results or realised that most consumers are untrusting of influencer recommendations.

This may surprise you, but I somewhat agree with you. I have seen brands spend thousands of dollars on influencer marketing only to feel incredibly disappointed because it wasn't effective. I've also overheard influencers talking about not liking a product but still promoting it because the brand payment was high. It really didn't instil much trust in me about those influencers.

So, why in the world am I writing a whole chapter on them? Because the influencer marketing strategy that we used to know is dead, but there are new, fresh strategies that work, all of which will propel some businesses into cult brands in the next few years. These strategies are also going to boost your brand awareness.

With the right influencer marketing tactics, you can access your target market from another entry point — most of whom have never heard of your brand before. Let's start with the basics.

How much should you pay for an influencer?

While it is quite nuanced and varies from influencer to influencer, there are some clear measurement tools that will help you understand what the costs will be.

Many marketers separate influencers into groups such as micro, mid-tier, macro and mega influencers, but that only refers to their follower count and isn't a great indicator of their charge rates. We can use this as a starting point when looking for influencers, but some rates may fall far outside these ranges depending on the specific influencer and their engagement rate.

Here are some rough rules of thumb for Instagram and TikTok. These are based on my experience with other brands that I have worked with who have worked with influencers across multiple platforms.

- Instagram

    - Nano influencers (1000–10000 followers): free–$800 per post

    - Micro influencers (10001–50000 followers): $800–$2500 per post

    - Mid-tier influencers (50001–500000 followers): $2000–$10000 per post

    - Macro influencers (500001–1000000 followers): $7500–$20000 per post

- Mega influencers (1 000 000+ followers): $18 000+ per post

- TikTok:

  - Nano influencers (1000–10 000 followers): $1000+ per post

  - Micro influencers (10,001–50 000 followers): $2500+ per post

  - Mid-tier influencers (50 001–500 000 followers): $5,000+ per post

  - Macro influencers (500 001–1 000 000 followers): $8000+ per post

  - Mega influencers 1 000 000+ followers): $15 000+ per post

Keep in mind that there are multiple factors that also affect their rates, such as usage rights, exclusivity, agency fees, campaign length, posting bundles and 'link in bio'.

Understanding the add-on fees

Usage rights refer to the agreement between your brand and an influencer, where the influencer will allow you to use their content across other marketing channels for a set period of time, and usually for an extra fee. You may want to use their content on your website or in your paid advertising. Generally, influencers charge about 30 per cent of their posting fee for usage fees (per month of usage).

If you want to make sure that the influencer doesn't work with one of your competitors within a certain timeframe, you can add in an *exclusivity clause*. Because this may stop them from obtaining other brand deals, the influencer may charge an extra fee for exclusivity.

Many influencers are represented by *agencies* or *managers* who will charge additional fees. On average, the agency will charge 15 per cent on top of the set fee, plus taxes.

If you need content *urgently*, the influencer can prioritise your content, but it may come at a cost. This is because what would usually take a longer amount of time to prepare, record and edit a video will be done in much less time.

If you want the influencer to add your *website link to their bio*, this may also come with an extra fee. Many influencers will add it as part of their package for a short amount of time but be prepared for some to add an extra charge.

How to find the right influencers

When scrolling through any social media platform, it feels like influencers are everywhere. But the minute you try and find the right influencer to market your business, you, frustratingly, can't find anyone. Luckily, I'm going to give you four easy ways to find them.

1. Old-school hunting

2. TikTok Creative Center and TikTok Creator Marketplace

3. Modash

4. GoAffPro

1. OLD-SCHOOL HUNTING

To this day, after many years of being in business, I still believe that old-school hunting is the best way to find influencers for your business. Old-school hunting involves scrolling through Instagram, YouTube and TikTok to find suitable influencers, but also searching for specific hashtags or topics.

Chances are, you already follow influencers who are related to your industry. Start there. Look at their accounts and look at their 'lookalike' influencers to find a match.

As you show interest in a certain industry or topic, each social platform will start serving you targeted content. Scrolling through this content will not only help you find influencers, but it's entertaining too!

2. TIKTOK CREATIVE CENTER AND TIKTOK CREATOR MARKETPLACE

These two tools were created by TikTok and they are a fantastic way to find the right TikTok creators. TikTok Creative Center allows you to search for and filter creators by country, industry and number of followers. TikTok Creator Marketplace allows you to sign up as a brand and run campaigns to find influencers. You can either reach out to them directly via the platform or have an open application process where content creators can apply to work with you.

These are both free tools.

3. MODASH

Modash is a comprehensive influencer marketing platform. It's designed so brands can connect with influencers across platforms such as Instagram, YouTube and TikTok. Modash has a huge database of influencers and several tools for tracking engagement metrics.

You can search for influencers by country, number of followers, engagement rate and topic. It has the biggest database of influencers that I have come across.

Modash is a paid tool.

4. GOAFFPRO

This tool will turn your customers into your influencers. This is not your traditional influencer marketing strategy, but it needs a mention because it can work incredibly well to get you in front of more of your target market.

GoAffPro is an affiliate marketing program where customers and other content creators can sign up on your website, create content for you and earn a commission every time someone makes a purchase from their recommendation.

How it works:

- You sign up to GoAffPro.

- You set your commission: This is the amount of money you are willing to pay your customers if they refer someone to your store and they make a purchase — usually this is a certain percentage of sales. Commissions mostly sit between 5 and 20 per cent. The higher the commission, the more customers will be incentivised to take part.

- Put your affiliate link in your header or footer menu (something like 'Become an affiliate').

- Tell your audience about the link and the commission they can earn. You can do this through social media or email.

- Customers or content creators can click on the link and sign up to become an affiliate for your business.

- They post content on their social media channels, send an email to their own database or simply share the link with friends.

- If anyone buys from you using their affiliate link, they will earn a commission.

The best thing is that it is all done automatically! After it has been set up and is firing, there is minimal effort required from you on a daily basis.

GoAffPro is a free Shopify app.

Influencer strategies

Now that you've found the right influencers for your business, let's dive straight into my favourite influencer strategies. I'm going to skip over the traditional influencer strategy where they hold up a product and smile. Nine times out of ten, this strategy doesn't work anymore. So, let's get into some more creative and effective ways to use influencers for your business.

INFLUENCER STRATEGY 1: INFLUENCER CO-CREATION

This is by far the best influencer strategy that I have analysed. Influencer co-creation is the process where a brand will work with an influencer to co-create a product. The influencer has creative control over the design and the ingredients or materials.

For example, if you sell:

◆ activewear, the influencer could design a hoodie and a T-shirt

◆ candles, the influencer could choose their own signature scent

◆ jewellery, the influencer could design a pair of earrings.

The power in this strategy is the vested interest the influencer has in making this collaboration successful. Because they have created the product, they will feel a sense of ownership, and this makes for a fantastic partnership between them and the brand.

This style of collaboration used to only be viable for large companies, but small businesses are now utilising this strategy with incredible success. Take, for example, my good friends Claire and Georgia who started El&Ro Jewellery. They used the influencer co-creation strategy with Kate Jones (also known as Dedikated_Lifestyle) who at the time had 185000 followers on Instagram. This collaboration saw Kate design a complete range of jewellery for El&Ro, including earrings and necklaces. Kate spent weeks designing it under the guidance of Claire and Georgia.

During this time, they created a lot of BTS content and started to build hype around the new collection.

The idea was to tap into Kate's engaged audience and bring them into their TOFU. To make sure they didn't lose any momentum, they created a waitlist page on their website. Every piece of content that was created by the brand or by Kate led audiences to sign up to the waitlist for this new collection (with the promise that they would have first access when it launched). Their main goal was brand awareness.

And it worked. El&Ro gained over 3000 new followers and collected hundreds of new email addresses, even before the products were made.

To celebrate the prelaunch, Claire and Georgia held an intimate lunch with Kate, and allowed her to invite ten of her closest friends. As most of them were influencers themselves, the lunch led to dozens of posts tagging the brand. El&Ro gained hundreds more followers and increased the excitement and hype around the launch.

When the collection went live on their website, the revenue they made in the first six hours of the launch matched an entire month of regular sales, and the collection was completely sold out in two days. This influencer strategy was so successful, that they have implemented it three times with Kate and done more with other influencers.

I have also implemented this strategy with Hero Packaging over the last four years and, to date, it's been our most successful marketing strategy. We collaborated with artists and influencers (with large audiences) to create custom packaging.

One of my favourite collaborations was the campaign we did with Sarah Davidson from Seize the Yay and Spoonful of Sarah. We designed a padded compostable mailer with one of her favourite quotes printed on the front: 'If you can't do great things, do small things in a great way'. We gifted her 1000 of those mailers to use in her business and we sold the rest. Every time she posted, we received hundreds of followers, but we also got lots of people clicking through to our website.

Within a month, the mailers had sold out. We knew it was a winning strategy.

TIMEFRAME

This strategy usually takes months to plan and execute so you need to work backwards from your ideal launch date. Say, for example, you want your launch date to be in September, you need to consider:

- finding the right influencer and agreeing upon fees and deliverables (about one month)

- designing the product or range (about one month)

- manufacturing times (about two to three months)

- other miscellaneous operational wait times (about two to three weeks).

That means you need to start working on this campaign at the start of April.

CONTRACT AND NEGOTIATION

When contacting the influencer or influencer agency, you need to be specific about the requirements:

◆ What is the design process?

◆ What are the key dates?

◆ How many items do you want designed?

◆ How many social posts/stories are needed?

◆ Will you have an event for the launch?

◆ What percentage of sales will you provide?

SPECIFIC SUCCESS TACTICS

To make this strategy successful, you need to do a lot of the planning and setup in advance. Here are some tactics to ensure it performs well:

◆ Set up your waitlist page and connect your email platform so you can capture everyone who is interested.

◆ Plan out the content strategy (with and without the influencer).

◆ Have an in-person event to launch the product or collection and have the influencer invite people they know.

◆ At the time of launch, go live on Instagram or TikTok with the influencer to achieve as much brand exposure as possible.

When you try this strategy for the first time, you will see what worked well specifically for your business and how you can improve things next time. Make notes on this and keep them handy to perfect it over time.

INFLUENCER STRATEGY 2: INFLUENCER-INSPIRED COLLECTION, AKA THE LAZY INFLUENCER METHOD

This strategy is quick, easy and has a huge impact on brand awareness. The lazy influencer method is where you ask an influencer to pick their favourite products from your website and you name a collection after them. This strategy simply involves your existing products and no new products; hence, the lazy method!

You can use a big influencer or a number of smaller influencers who could be affiliates for your brand (this is where they receive a percentage of each sale). It incentivises them to post more about your brand because they receive something out of each sale.

The idea is to name the collection after the influencer without needing to send them free products. The only thing they need to do is go to your website and select their top three to ten products. Once you create the collection, you can add product badges to the images to say '[Influencer's] Top Picks'.

One of the best examples of this is Showpo collaborating with Flex Mami. Showpo is one of Australia's largest online fashion retailers and they sell a wide variety of women's clothing. Flex Mami, aka Lillian Ahenkan, is an influencer, DJ, author and style icon (more on Flex Mami in Chapter 29).

There was a time where she was always wearing plisse sets. She wore them in different colours and styled them in different ways. She had bought them all from Showpo. Showpo caught on to this and decided to name a collection after her: Flex Mami Collection. In that collection were 63 items that Flex picked as her favourite pieces of clothing.

The collection was such a great strategy for Showpo because Flex owned an audience on social media who loved her style and may never have purchased from Showpo before. Showpo was able to access a new group of people who were also part of their target market.

> **Tip**
>
> Try and choose influencers who have already bought from you before. Not only can you add the products they have bought previously to the collection, but they are more likely to say yes because they already love you.

INFLUENCER STRATEGY 3: THE EXPERT

The best influencers are the ones who aren't officially influencers. The best ones are the people who have skills, authority and credibility in an industry or on a certain topic.

Let's look at my mum as an example. My mum's a doctor and is probably the biggest medical influencer in the suburb in which she works. Many of her patients have been visiting her for over 20 years, and they wholeheartedly trust her medical advice. If she says to exercise more, they do it. If she says that they need to take a particular vitamin, they take it.

She is an original influencer. Unfortunately, she never wanted to be on Instagram so my dreams of her being a famous influencer were squashed.

But the concept of the expert influencer has always stuck with me. There are experts in every industry who are creating content about that specific industry on social media. They usually don't have a huge following, but they are either trying to educate people or are showing people what it's like in that industry.

This strategy works really well for people whose audience isn't necessarily large, but is very niched, and who follows them because of their skillset.

For example, let's say you sell medical scrubs. You could target people on Instagram and TikTok who are nurses and send them free products. In this case, you would search for a hashtag such as #nursesoftiktok and find nurses who would love your scrubs.

Filter the search results by recent results and 'most liked'. Look through all the nurse creators and find those who would be a good fit for your brand. Reach out to them via email or DMs to start collaborating with them.

Even if it is a gifted collaboration (where you don't pay them to post, you just gift them your product), make sure you ask if they have a rate for content usage in advertising. The type of content that will be produced from these experts and authority figures will be some of the best for your brand. You want to be able to use these for your Meta and TikTok ads.

A very successful example of this 'expert' strategy was used by CeraVe. Let's look at their case study.

CERAVE CASE STUDY

The objective: CeraVe have had rapid growth in the last few years, and they wanted to build upon this success in local markets for women aged 18 to 34.

The strategy: CeraVe decided to hire skin experts in different countries to create content on TikTok, specifically talking about the unique benefits of its essential ceramide ingredients. Each expert was asked to create two pieces of content that would be used later by the brand for in-feed ads. This brand-awareness strategy leveraged their expertise and followers to generate demand for CeraVe in their specific markets.

The results: The campaign was a major success, driving 13 million video views and an 84 per cent uplift in brand recall. In Australia, there was a 29 per cent uplift in CeraVe preference over competitors.

INFLUENCER STRATEGY 4: GO GUERRILLA

As attention spans become shorter and shorter, nothing stands out like a clever guerrilla marketing tactic. In 2021, at the height of COVID lockdowns, I saw one of the best small-business guerrilla marketing campaigns play out.

At the time, two boys known on social media as The Inspired Unemployed were growing fast on social media. The Inspired Unemployed is a viral comedy duo formed in 2019 by Matt Ford and Jack Steele. Best known for their Australian satire, they had grown to over 1 million followers in 2021.

In September that year, they were stuck in hotel quarantine for a week. As many people were also stuck at home during this time, they were glued to their phones and watching the boys for a good laugh. One day, the boys received a package and it was a hammock. That's when the fun started. Over a period of five days, The Inspired Unemployed boys started receiving packages and notes from someone, but they had no idea who it was. In one note, they were told to look outside their window only to see a man in his budgie smugglers (bathers) swinging on a hammock with a hat covering his face (and identity) on the street below.

They received notes with tasks that they needed to complete to get more gifts, as well as walkie talkies so they could talk to this mysterious 'Hammock Man'. The boys posted the notes and packages to their social media accounts and their audience was engaged in watching the events unfold. They were all curious about who 'Hammock Man' was. Even Channel 9 visited Hammock Man to try and get the inside scoop.

On the fifth day, Hammock Man finally revealed himself to be Jaryd Leibbrandt, the founder of Nakie (a camping and outdoor product brand). He sent the notes and packages to entertain people and bring joy at a time when people felt isolated and alone.

Overnight, Nakie gained over 30000 new followers and was featured in podcasts from The Inspired Unemployed to Happy Hour with Lucy and Nikki. The guerrilla marketing tactic that barely cost them anything gained them incredible brand awareness.

Here's how you can use influencers to do guerrilla marketing:

- ◆ Find an influencer you would love to work with.

- ◆ Learn everything about them, from their hobbies to their favourite food. Get a complete understanding of something they would love to share on their social accounts.

- ◆ Don't send them a product — send a shareable experience (one that they can't help posting about).

- ◆ Try and send them multiple experiences to build up curiosity and excitement.

- ◆ Do the final reveal and talk about why you did it.

Tip

Try and find something that has recently happened to them that they have been talking about, such as getting married, having a baby, buying a caravan, travelling to India or writing a book, and try to weave your product and campaign around that. The more tailored your guerrilla tactic is to the specific influencer, the more likely they will be to talk about it.

INFLUENCER STRATEGY 5: GIVEAWAYS

This is an old-school approach to marketing. It is one of the only influencer strategies that has stood the test of time. Remember, we are still talking about TOFU strategies, so we are trying to build as much brand awareness as possible, as well as gain more followers who are in your target market. This strategy is a fantastic way to do just that.

Coconut Bowls, an online store selling handcrafted coconut bowls, generated over 40 000 email subscribers within a month by utilising a viral giveaway strategy, and it only cost them $1000.

Let's dive into a case study on how they did this.

COCONUT BOWLS CASE STUDY

The objective: Coconut bowls wanted to generate email sign ups and social engagement with their bowls.

The strategy: Leveraging their Instagram account (where most of their followers are), they staged a giveaway with a handful of health- and sustainability-focused influencers.

The tools: Coconut Bowls used Instagram, Vyper and Klaviyo to run the giveaway.

The prize: They chose a high-value item (a Vitamix) and their own products (the bowls).

How it was executed: Coconut Bowls and their influencers announced the big giveaway at the same time by posting an image to their respective channels. Their audiences were directed to a landing page built by Vyper where they learnt more about the giveaway and had to enter their email address to be in with a chance to win. This form was created by Klaviyo and embedded on the landing page.

The landing page encouraged entrants to share the giveaway to other platforms or upload a video of their coconut bowl to earn more entries.

The results: The campaign had 222 263 page views and Coconut Bowls received 37 703 new Instagram followers and 41 820 email addresses. The landing page conversion rate was 18 per cent.

This giveaway was so successful due to a few key reasons:

- The prize was of high value.

- The influencers were selected because they closely represented the values of the brand.

- They optimised the landing page to encourage further engagement and sharing.

INFLUENCER STRATEGY 6: EXPERIENTIAL EVENT

Having an in-person event, such as a meet and greet, lunch, popup or activation, where people can meet their favourite influencer and also take away free products, is a guaranteed way to get more eyeballs on your brand and more followers.

By leveraging the audiences of influencers at your events, you not only get more brand awareness, but it gives your brand credibility in your category. One of the best ways to implement this is for a launch or prelaunch event.

When you are about to launch your new product or collection, having an influencer event can generate buzz around your brand. You can do this by inviting a few influencers and some of your loyal customers so they can see and feel the collection/product in person.

The idea is to get the customers to talk about it on social media and mention your brand, while also receiving exposure from the influencers. A winning tactic is to try and build a waitlist for the new product/collection (similar to what El&Ro Jewellery and Dedikated_ Lifestyle did on page 50), so it is beneficial if you and the influencers have a link to the waitlist page in the link in the bio.

A great example of this is when Wildfire Shoes invited Brittney Saunders and Flex Mami to their prelaunch event. Brittney and Flex did a Q&A on stage and then mingled with the crowd of customers. This generated a lot of buzz on social media and an increase of thousands of followers for Wildfire Shoes.

INFLUENCER STRATEGY 7: WHITELISTING

Whitelisting is when a brand promotes a video from an influencer's account — the influencer needs to grant the brand permission to use their social media account to pay for the ad. For example, if I create a video on TikTok about my Sony headphones, Sony can use my video as an ad. To audiences on TikTok, the ad looks like it's running from my account, but Sony is actually running it through their ads manager.

There are so many advantages to whitelisting:

- You can put money behind an organic video that is already doing well.

- You can target the exact audience you want to see that video.

- It looks like it is coming from the influencer, not the brand, so has more credibility.

- You can add CTA buttons on the video.

HOW CAN BRANDS WHITELIST INFLUENCERS ON FACEBOOK AND INSTAGRAM?

This is all done through Meta Business Manager. You can Google how to set this up, but you need to make sure that the influencer has a Meta Business Manager account that is correctly linked to their Facebook and Instagram pages.

You will also need to add the influencer as a business partner, and they will need to provide you with their Business Manager ID.

Alternatively, you can use a tool, such as Leadsie, to do this for you. It will be able to access the influencers' posts and you can choose to promote one of them from there.

HOW CAN BRANDS WHITELIST INFLUENCERS ON TIKTOK?

These ads are also known as Spark Ads. Whitelisting TikTok videos is much simpler than Meta videos. Once a creator has posted the video, they can go into their settings, and share the ad's authorisation code with you. Once the video is authorised, you can create your spark ad. You can create this in the same way as creating any other TikTok ad (see chapter 11).

As I started to grow my following on TikTok, I was asked to do various types of influencer campaigns for brands. Most of the time, if they are running ads, they will ask to do a whitelisted ad from my account. Here is an example of one I did:

Google created a new tool called Duet AI, and they paid me to create a video on TikTok explaining how to use it. Three days after posting it, they whitelisted my video. The video ran as an ad from my TikTok account, not Google's account. Over a few weeks, this ad generated over 239 000 views, 5100 shares and 1600 people had signed up to the Duet AI tool.

The 5100 shares indicate that those 5100 people had not heard about Google's Duet AI before and deemed it interesting enough to share with others. Google now had access to 1600 new business owners to promote the Duet AI tool and other business tools.

Whitelisting is a fantastic way to gain brand awareness.

CHAPTER 8

TOFU strategy #3: Digital PR

Hero Packaging is arguably Australia's most recognised e-commerce packaging company. Much of that recognition is a result of digital public relations (PR). Hero Packaging has been featured in hundreds of online publications from Smart Company to the official Shopify blog, and we were also on SBS and Channel 7. This made us a category leader in Australia, built trust with our business customers (from small businesses to large national retailers) and allowed us to get in front of people at all levels in an organisation.

For any business, getting the right PR will allow you to cut through the noise in a crowded market and have prominence over your competitors, and will garner trust in your brand. Remember when a cold audience sees you everywhere, it builds familiarity and trust with your brand. This leads to your brand being part of their consideration set when making purchasing decisions.

How to get PR for your brand

I knew from the beginning that I needed some sort of PR in my business, but I was also quite aware that hiring an agency would be expensive. So, I looked into DIY ways of getting PR. That's when I stumbled across Linkby.

Linkby as a DIY tool

Linkby is a PR platform that helps brands get more editorial coverage via a cost-per-click (CPC) model. Let me break it down for you:

Linkby has over 250 media publishers on its platform, including *Buzzfeed, Daily Mail,* News Corp, Refinery29 and Nine News. You can sign up as an advertiser on the platform and choose which publications you would like to be featured in. You write a pitch for your story or what your new product launch is and attach relevant photos.

As it is a CPC model, you must choose how much you are willing to pay per click (this is when the article has been published and readers click through to your website). Usually, the CPC is about $2.50. The higher the CPC, the more beneficial it is for a publisher to run the story on their website.

You need to also select your overall budget — this is the maximum spend per publication. For example, if you set your CPC to $2.50 and your overall budget to $2500, then you will get a maximum number of 1000 clicks. This means that 1000 people who have probably never heard of your brand will have clicked through to your website to look at your products.

While $2500 sounds like a lot of money, you most likely won't get anywhere near 1000 clicks. You may get about 100 clicks, which means you will pay $250 for an article published in a prominent media outlet, and you also receive 100 new people to your site. It's a pretty great concept.

When I used Linkby for Hero Packaging, I got featured in *Broadsheet* as well as *Urban List* and it cost me $500 in total. Those articles were fantastic for us because they also boosted our SEO and drove incremental traffic long after they were published. We also got to use those features in our content and advertising.

Tip

You must have a good PR angle and a good story to tell. Just because you are paying a publisher doesn't mean they will definitely pick up the story. Angles that work well include:

◆ seasonal sales/discounts

◆ gift ideas during peak gifting times

◆ new product launch

◆ influencer collaboration

◆ revenue/sales growth figures.

PROS OF LINKBY

◆ It is easier than manually finding media contacts and sending a press release.

◆ It is a one-stop PR shop with access to hundreds of publishers.

◆ It has a global network with publications in multiple countries.

CONS OF LINKBY

- ◆ It is a CPC model so it's similar to paying for an advertisement.

- ◆ It is a brand-awareness tool, so while there may be clicks to your website (that you will pay for), you may not get the sales to cover the outlay.

HARO: Help a Reporter Out

Another great tool is HARO, or Help a Reporter Out, which is widely used by journalists to find stories to publish. Journalists are usually asked to write about certain topics or trending stories. They send their questions or topics to HARO, and HARO sends an email to all the business owners and bloggers that are subscribed.

If there is a topic that a business owner has expertise in, they can write directly to that journalist with their answer. It essentially connects journalists and bloggers with relevant expertise to help journalists meet their demanding deadlines and enables brands to tell their stories. It's a straightforward pitching process that allows sources to find topics related to their expertise, industry or experience, while allowing journalists and bloggers to spend more time writing and less time sourcing.

PROS OF HARO

- ◆ It is a free service.

- ◆ You get to write about topics that you know journalists are looking to write about.

- ◆ It pushes PR opportunities straight into your inbox and offers media opportunities for various industries and topics.

- ◆ It's an easy way to get in contact with reporters and journalists, who might contact you directly in future for similar topics.

CONS OF HARO

◆ There are an overwhelming number of emails with different topics. I was receiving two to three a day, and I eventually stopped looking at them.

◆ It is a very old-school method to get published — there is no platform to track your responses or articles that have been published.

◆ There is a lack of feedback from journalists.

Engaging a PR agency

A few years after starting Hero, we hired a PR agency. It was a big expense for us at the time, but I felt like it was the right time. We had had a great run with Hero, but I could see many small competitors popping up. They were copying our products, our website, our content and our ads. If I created a piece of content, they would create the same piece of content. If I created a new product, six months later they would do the same thing.

I knew Hero had to stand out. I did my research and found a PR agent who was highly recommended. After starting with her, Hero's online presence significantly increased. From TV, to news sites, to podcasts — we were everywhere. Getting this exposure boosted our brand recognisability. We became the go-to, trusted packaging brand in Australia.

Even though we continued to sell the same products, we had authority in the space because our PR agent put us forward for sustainability and other knowledge-based articles. We continued for a year with the agency, but at the end of 2022, when our profitability wasn't where we wanted it to be, we had to make marketing cuts. So, we stopped working with an agency.

However, the year-long media exposure meant that I didn't need to chase opportunities — publications started to reach out to me organically for opinion pieces and my brand story. The PR ball was rolling, and it no longer needed pushing.

Tip

If you want to use a PR agency for published articles as well as influencer/PR gifting and in-real-life (IRL) activations (e.g., physically handing out products at a site), then remember that the agency fee is only part of the cost. A good activation can cost in excess of $20 000, and PR-gifting campaigns also have costs like your product, packaging and shipping.

Be mindful of exactly what you want the agency to do and talk to them about pricing from the start. My agency cost $4400 per month — most will charge anywhere from $2000 to $20 000 per month.

PROS OF A PR AGENCY

♦ It is a done-for-you service and requires minimal effort on your part.

♦ They have established connections with media and influencers.

♦ They will create a comprehensive strategy based on your brand, products and what they think will get noticed.

♦ Having a constant stream of articles written about your brand will help make you a category leader.

CONS OF A PR AGENCY

♦ It is relatively expensive.

♦ You will not see an immediate return on your investment as it is a brand-awareness tool, not an online conversion tool.

◆ You may need to fork out additional funds for events, activations, PR packs and influencer gifts.

Winning awards

Wouldn't it be lovely to refer to your brand as an 'award-winning business'? Even though winning awards is a vanity measure, it does also come with the added benefit of getting exposure and credibility for your brand. Awards are also newsworthy. Every time Hero Packaging has won an award, we have been featured in three to four online articles.

Many of the awards are run by publishers themselves, so if you are a finalist or win, you will get free PR for your business.

There are two parts to applying for awards: the fee and the questions.

THE FEE

You need to be aware that when you apply for an award, it will most likely have a cost associated with it. This to encourage only serious entries (and because many of these companies use awards as an extra revenue stream). It can range from $50 to $2000, depending on the calibre of award. When choosing which awards you want to apply for, look at the cost and pick wisely. For me, it always comes down to the calibre and industry recognition of that award, as well as the potential for PR opportunities.

THE QUESTIONS

I have applied for many awards for my businesses, and unless the award is in a specific category (e.g., best equestrian business), many of the questions are very similar. I have compiled the most commonly asked questions in award applications. I want you to take some time and write your answers to each question and save them so you have easy access to them whenever you apply. Many of your answers should already be in your brag book as discussed at the start of this book!

- Tell us about your business.

- Tell us about you. Why did you start this business?

- What makes your brand different from others?

- What are your key growth drivers?

- What are your business achievements in the last 12 months? This is where you talk about:

  - financial achievements

  - collaborations and partnerships

  - innovative practices

  - business expansion

  - increase in staff

  - increase in turnover and/or profit

  - industry recognition.

- Tell us about your marketing initiatives.

- Do you give back to the community? How?

- Why are you a leader in your space?

- What is the future of your business?

- What environmental impact does your business have?

- How do you foster a positive team culture?

- Why should you win [award]?

Tip

Some of these have a limit of 100 to 150 words, so write a long version and a short version for each question. Keep a record of all answers so you build a bank of answers to easily apply for awards next time.

Q&A with Rachael Wilde, founder of tbh Skincare

Rachael Wilde is a master of brand awareness and if you haven't heard of her, you have almost certainly heard of – or seen, or used or talked about – the skincare brand she co-founded in March 2020.

tbh Skincare, the new-age skincare range beloved by celebrities, including Abbie Chatfield, Oliva Molly Rogers and Keira Maguire, has been a market-disrupting addition to the beauty landscape from the very first sale of its Acne Hack Spot Treatment. Three years on, the product continues to enjoy a cult-favourite status, with one Acne Hack Spot Treatment snapped up every four minutes.

I asked her how she used brand-awareness strategies to create one of Australia's fastest-growing skincare brands.

How did you initially create awareness about tbh Skincare? What specific strategies did you find most effective in the early stages of your business?

> When I started tbh Skincare in 2020, the skincare market was already saturated, so I knew I had to make my business stand apart from other brands by having a unique tone of voice. At the time, skincare brands were pushing the scientific angle, so I decided to cut through the noise by using a fun, cheeky and sassy brand personality, and I coupled this with inclusivity and positivity.
>
> Another thing we did right off the bat was invest in Facebook ads. I knew that an organic social strategy was not going to be

enough for consistent brand awareness, so I put money into Facebook ads to target new audiences.

How do you create brand awareness now? Do your brand awareness strategies look a lot different to what you were doing when you started?

We have been working with two major Australian influencers: Abbie Chatfield and Olivia Molly Rogers. We don't just use them for one-off posts. Because of our genuine relationship with them and their love for the brand, they are on 12-month retainers. They have managed to get us in front of tens of thousands of our ideal target market and have managed to significantly increase our exposure as a reputable, but cool skincare brand.

Another strategy we use is PR. This is a winning strategy for us because it not only gets us noticed by millions of people, but gives us credibility and authority in this industry. In 2023, we had a media mention every two days! To do this, we use a PR agency on a monthly retainer.

One thing that hasn't changed for us is prioritising social content. In fact, this is a huge generator of new audiences. We have spent over three years analysing and perfecting what content works and what has the highest likelihood of going viral, and I think we have done a pretty good job of it!

Tell me more about your organic social media strategy. How can you make something go viral?

We have key pillars that we use to create viral content. One of the pillars is 'timely' content. This is where we take something that is trending or in the news; for example, when the *Barbie* movie was released, the hype around it was insane, so I dressed up as Margot Robbie and went to popular hotspots around Sydney—I even had a chaperone and a crew of people who followed me around to make it seem real. We captured people's reactions as I walked past and collated them into a video. This video received 2.6 million views and nearly 152 000 likes. This video went viral because it was based around a trending topic, and because it lent itself to a lot of opinionated comments.

Another pillar is 'Behind the scenes', but it's not your regular BTS content. The social media girls will film us in a meeting where they propose funny and over-the-top marketing ideas to get my reaction. These videos go viral every single time because their ideas get more and more ludicrous, and also because they are real and unscripted.

How do you and your team come up with content ideas like this?

I have a team of three content creators and one of the main things I did when I handed over the reins was to create a space where they could brainstorm and feel empowered to make creative decisions. I don't give them rules and guidelines — we have content pillars that they work with to create funny, controversial and shareable content. We have realised that reach is purely based on the entertainment value of the videos, nothing else.

As a brand, I took the risk of not creating product-focused content. We treat our channel as though it's a personal page where our audience can relate to us on a human level, rather than on a product level. While this goes against pushing for conversions and sales, it leads to having a strong brand presence on TikTok and engaging users to try our product simply because we are cool and funny.

Recently you were on the front cover of the Australian Financial Review *(AFR)—an incredible achievement! What are most publications looking for when it comes to a good story?*

Publications want a fresh perspective on a given topic. When we pitch tbh, we try and really stand out from other brands by going against the grain and doing things differently. For example, we decided to launch our brand into Priceline and Coles when everyone had told us to aim for high-end retailers, such as Mecca and Sephora. But we knew we wanted to be accessible, and we wanted the volume, so we turned those warnings into green flags and took a risk. It really paid off for us, and publications love to learn about that.

Of course, all publications are different, but there are three key things that they look for: popular influencers who have used your product, growth stats and financial figures, and a great founder story.

With AFR, specifically, they like facts and figures and protectable IP, such as patents. We have a patent on our technology and that is one of our biggest strengths. Not many skincare brands have this, so it gives us an edge.

Based on your experience, what key advice would you give small business owners about getting more brand awareness and new customers?

Carve out something unique—you must have uniqueness in your product, tone of voice or story in order for people to take an interest in your brand. Try and be different to everyone else, because to get more eyeballs, you need to stand out from your competitors. Everyone is fighting for attention, so make sure you capture it from the outset.

Another piece of advice is to repeat your message constantly. A common mistake I see business owners make is that they try and create new messaging around their brand to make it interesting. This dilutes your brand message because when you are creating top-of-funnel content, it will be new people that see your content all the time. Don't feel the need to change it. Whatever your uniqueness and your messaging is, say it consistently in different places because this leads to better brand recall. This consistent communication strategy will also mean that, as more and more people hear about your brand, your brand will be known for one thing. This is very powerful.

CHAPTER 9

TOFU strategy #4: Brand collaborations

The best way to explain brand collaborations is with a quick example. Imagine you run an online candle brand. You are trying to figure out a creative way to tap into new customers and get brand exposure. You see cool brand collaborations like KitchenAid x Alemais and you wonder if it could work for smaller businesses. You find a popular bakery and ask them to collaborate with you on a limited-edition chocolate cookie candle.

Fast forward a few months, and the collaboration is a reality. Your exclusive candle, co-created with the famous bakery, is making waves and lots of new people are coming to your website every day. You have also gained lots of new followers on social media and hundreds of people have signed up for the next launch. This is the power of brand collaboration in action, gaining each other's audiences and creating something memorable.

A successful brand collaboration is more than just sharing logos; it also creates experiences that hold significance with shared target audiences. This is why brand collaborations are important for brand awareness:

- ◆ When the brands get together, they reach the other's customers. It's a win-win situation where both share the spotlight.

- ◆ It creates more buzz. When two companies collaborate, people notice. They talk about it with friends and post about it on social media, and the excitement spreads like wildfire. This creates a buzz that's hard to match with regular product launches.

- ◆ It builds trust and credibility. If your favourite brand teams up with another one you've never tried, you're more likely to give it a shot. It's like your friend vouching for someone new.

Types of brand collaborations

There are numerous ways to partner with another brand:

Product co-creation

You are essentially creating a product that embodies both brands. An example of this is the Gelato Messina collaboration with Sundae Body. Sundae Body created its shower foams with some of Gelato Messina's best-selling flavours, including lamington and strawberries and cream.

Not-for-profit

This is where you can collaborate with a not-for-profit to donate the proceeds of certain products. An example of this is when Hero Packaging collaborated with an Indigenous artist to create packaging that represented First Nations people. We paid the artist to design the artwork, and also donated 20 per cent of the proceeds of this packaging to Children's Ground, an Indigenous charity. The best thing about this collaboration was that we were able to bring the awareness of First Nations culture to our audience, and the artist and charity were able to bring awareness of sustainability to their audience.

Sponsorship

Sponsorship is a brand collaboration where a brand provides financial support or resources to another company, like a sports team or a non-profit organisation, for example. In return, the sponsoring brand receives exposure, branding opportunities and access to the sponsored partner's audience, which helps boost brand visibility and build associations with a particular cause or activity.

Cross-promotion bundle

Cross-promotion is a brand collaboration where two or more brands join forces to promote each other's products or services and tap into new customer segments to expand their reach. To do this, they typically use joint marketing campaigns, discounts, bundled offerings or shared advertising efforts. An example of this was when the iconic brands Go-To Skincare, Frank Body and Sand & Sky released a limited-edition box full of their bestsellers. It was promoted across all of their platforms. It was a win-win-win.

Q&A with Jess Ruhfus, founder of Collabosaurus

Jess Ruhfus is no stranger to entrepreneurship. From building an English-tutoring business in her teens to the acquisition of her Collabosaurus software in 2023, Jess is currently building No.2 Co, a natural and stylish bathroom fragrance solution. These innovative toilet drops have garnered attention from publications like *The Daily Mail, Broadsheet*, Apartment Therapy, Domain and *Body & Soul* magazine.

Her recently acquired venture, Collabosaurus, facilitates marketing collaborations and partnerships for over 10 500+ brands. Drawing on her background in fashion publicity and small business marketing education, Collabosaurus bootstrapped its way to working with industry heavyweights, such as Porsche, ASOS, Bondi Sands and Marks & Spencer, under her leadership. Jess won the 2019 B&T 30 Under 30 award for Entrepreneurship and has been the keynote speaker at numerous events, including for *Vogue*, Microsoft, General Assembly and Apple.

You have been in the brand collaboration space for a decade! Do you think brand collaborations still have the same impact and success today?

Definitely. In fact, I think brand collaborations can be even more successful now. When I first started in brand collaborations about a decade ago, I had to do so much education for business owners because it was a very new marketing strategy. Now, brand collaborations are everywhere and used by large brands to small businesses.

Brands now also understand that collaborations aren't just giveaways — there are so many ways to have success with them, including activations, events, email swaps, guerrilla marketing and so much more.

One of the best things about brand collaborations is that you can leverage owned, earned and paid channels in one. When you look at any other marketing strategy, it's usually siloed into one. For example, ads are paid, organic content is earned, and website optimisation is owned. Collabs can use all three and they are usually much cheaper to execute.

What are the best types of brand collaborations that a small business can implement?

The traditional method is, obviously, a giveaway, but there's so much more you can do.

But before you look at the types of collaborations, you need to be clear about what you want to achieve. Do you want sales? Email subscribers? Brand awareness with a new audience? Fresh content? Getting clear on the goal will allow you to choose what type of collaboration will work best, and I like to break it out into three main parts: social media, product or events/experiences.

For social media, brands can do a content series where two or more brands create a limited-edition series of educational or entertaining content, or a competition where the brands offer equal-value prizes to gain followers or email addresses.

For product, brands can do a gift with purchase (where one brand offers their products to be added as a gift with purchase to the collaborating brand's customers), co-branded bundles (such as the Tiffany and Nike runner), samples, or shopper marketing (in retail stores). A great example of shopper marketing is when KIC partnered with Frank Body and gifted a free four-week membership to the KIC app if a customer bought a Frank Body product from Coles. This benefited both brands as customers were more incentivised to buy Frank Body, and KIC could get more awareness and signups.

For events/experiences, there are so many creative things brands can do. I did a collaboration for my brand No.2 with a business that hosted a lunch for e-commerce founders. The lunch was held in a luxurious mansion in Sydney and the attendees were all women in business. I did a bathroom takeover where I placed 30 full-sized bottles of my product in the bathroom with a note saying: 'Please take one — it's free'. This collaboration generated a lot of buzz about my brand at the lunch because I only placed 30 bottles in the bathroom, but there were 50 women at the lunch. There was a lot of chatter amongst the women because some missed out on a bottle. Many of the women asked how to get one and started Googling my brand, and some even purchased bottles online while they were at the lunch. It was one of the most effective marketing strategies I've ever done.

Tell me about your favourite brand collab in the last year. What were the results of that campaign?

I have so many! I absolutely loved the Kitchen Aid and Alemais collaboration, where Alemais designed an Australian landscape-inspired print for Kitchen Aid's Artisan Stand Mixer. This collaboration worked because of their joint love of quality craftsmanship and very similar audiences. They are also brands that have a mid-to premium price point in their industries. The collection sold out very quickly. They also ran a giveaway that reached over 500 000 people. To top it off, they held a dinner party event and invited customers to attend. This was also featured in nine major publications. It was a beautifully executed collaboration.

What is your best advice for business owners who want to do a brand collaboration this year?

If you haven't already tried a collaboration, just do it! Business owners tend to put collabs in the 'too hard' basket because they are unsure of the returns, but a good collaboration can be incredibly powerful for a business to grow or get exposure to a new audience.

Make collaborations part of your marketing mix and do them often. Test different types to see which one works best for your brand. For my brand, No.2, events and experiences have been the most effective and I'll be doing many more this year.

CHAPTER 10

TOFU strategy #5: TikTok

Let me tell you the story about how a local brand captured the attention of Oprah Winfrey on TikTok.

Beysis is an Australian brand that creates lifestyle products that are eco-friendly, with their most famous product being their personalised water bottles. In 2020, the founders at Beysis saw how brands on TikTok were experiencing rapid growth, and loved that it created a level playing field for all businesses. They recognised that, even without a following, videos could reach thousands (and sometimes millions) of viewers.

They started to post consistent content every day, mostly BTS footage of their business. They created 'pack an order with us' videos, office-tour videos and meet-the-team videos. They truly embraced the platform's demand for less-polished, high-engagement content. By doing this, they achieved an organic click-through rate that was higher than industry averages and gained a 5000 per cent increase in views within a few weeks. During this time, Oprah Winfrey bought one of their bottles and coined it 'the perfect bottle'. Their reaction video to Oprah talking about the bottle gave Beysis a huge boost in brand awareness.

This is the beauty of TikTok—you never know who will see your content.

TikTok is not a social media platform, it is a broadcast platform. While you can build a community on TikTok to an extent, I want you to treat it like a billboard—a brand-led, one-way messaging platform. Every video you create on that platform will be seen by new people (i.e., people who don't follow you). Whether you get 200 views or 1 million views on any video, many of those are people who have never heard about your brand. That's why TikTok is one of my favourite tools to get brand awareness.

In fact, TikTok holds a very special place in my heart. I first started creating content on the platform in 2021. The majority of TikTok content at the time was dancing videos and trends. Business content was minimal, so I didn't really know how to start on the platform. All I knew was that I didn't want to dance.

I spent weeks trying to figure out the algorithm and wrote down some video ideas. In all honesty, I was probably procrastinating because I was too scared to start. But one night, I remember seeing a video of a lady who told a story about getting fired from her job and starting a marketing agency. It was filmed in bad lighting at night, but it was so engaging. When I looked to the right, I saw that she had over 2000 likes. I kept revisiting that video because that was the type of content I knew I could create: low-fi, educational and face-to-camera content. When I revisited the video the next day, it had over 10000 likes. That was the lightbulb moment for me. I knew I had to start creating.

I had heard some people say that, in order to grow, I needed to create three to four videos a day. So, that's exactly what I did. Without fail, I created three to four pieces of content specific to TikTok. Some got 200 views, some got 500 views. The numbers didn't bother me; I just kept going.

I spoke about how I started my businesses, mistakes I had made, Canva tips and tricks, and marketing hacks. Whenever I ran out of content ideas, I would open up a business book and talk about a marketing concept I had read. A few weeks into creating content, I woke up to 10 000 views on one of my videos and over 1000 new followers. But the best part was that three people booked me for a one-on-one call with them — my first three business clients.

As the days went on, I continued to create three to four videos a day, but I also kept an eye on my semi-viral video. Within a week, it had reached 70 000 views and I booked another 11 one-on-one calls. It was at that point that I knew TikTok was going to be my winning marketing strategy.

For businesses, TikTok is a platform that allows for enormous reach, and has the potential to be your highest converting channel. However, creating engaging videos and understanding the algorithm takes time and a lot of testing.

Many business owners I speak to feel like they get stuck in what they call the '200-view jail', where their content never reaches more than 200 people. This is because TikTok hasn't deemed the content engaging enough to push it out to more people.

I am going to show you the best way to utilise TikTok for your business and how to get out of that 200-view jail once and for all.

There are a few tasks that I would like you to do before we start with TikTok strategies.

Hack your algorithm

The TikTok algorithm is the curated, personalised content that TikTok thinks you would like to watch. If you open the app and see Alix Earle putting on makeup while talking about her day, then it's because you've engaged with similar content before. If you see a duckling sitting on a puppy, TikTok knows you love cute things. It is dictated by what videos you have watched and engaged with in the past. Because of this, I want you to have two TikTok accounts so that you have two separate algorithms: one for your business and one for you personally. When you are browsing TikTok for entertainment, use your personal account. The funny memes and cute dogs should stay on your personal algorithm. You are going to use your business account to serve you content that is related to your industry/business/product/trends. This account is not for pleasure — it's a marketing tool and a spy tool.

Have a business account, not a creator account

Make sure that, for your brand, you have a business account on TikTok. There are quite a few reasons for this:

- While you can't use many of the trending sounds, you get access to thousands of commercial sounds. If you have a creator account for your business and then switch to a business account, all your videos that used trending sounds will not have sound anymore. Better to switch over sooner than later.

- You have access to more analytics and support.

- TikTok will give you access to tools and guides to help with your content creation.

- You have access to ads manager where you can eventually run paid ads.

Here are my top strategies for growing on TikTok as a business.

Watch TikTok intentionally

As I said before, you need to hack your algorithm. Let's say you sell hair clips. I want you to start engaging with hair content, makeup content, celebrity styling content and get-ready-with-me content. Essentially, you need to make a list of your target market's behaviours and interests and engage with that specific content.

To go a step further, use TikTok's search functionality (which is fantastic) and search for those interests. Filter the search by 'most liked' and by videos created in the last three months. Watch all of those videos and like them, comment on them and save them.

Not only will this give you inspiration for the type of content you can create, but it will also hack the algorithm to show you what you want to see as a business.

Think like a creator, not like a business

As business owners, our mindset is to sell more products. We go onto a platform like TikTok and create content for the sole purpose of getting everyone to look at our products and buy them. It's a natural thing to do. As you will soon figure out, if you haven't already, this approach will fail.

I'm not saying that you shouldn't showcase your products. I am saying you should weave it into a story or into incredibly engaging content. Your approach to TikTok should be like an influencer/content creator's approach to TikTok: entertaining, relatable, aspirational or educational.

Here are three tips when it comes to creating that content:

1. It's all about the hook

Firstly, 80 per cent of the success of your video is the hook — the first sentence/question or first three seconds of your video. You need to master the art of capturing attention from the second that someone scrolls to your video. When you are trying to find good hooks, have a look at videos from successful TikTok brands, such as Feastables, Mini Katana, See the Way I See and Strawberry Milk Mob.

2. Take note of the trends

Use trends where possible. If you are stuck for content ideas, jump on a trending sound or trending action. It's a quick way to increase your views. The way to find trends is to simply scroll through your feed and look at sounds that are used by multiple creators. Apply that trend to your business, product or industry.

3. Edit with CapCut

Use CapCut to edit your videos. CapCut is a video editing tool that is owned by TikTok, so the two tools work seamlessly together. CapCut also has loads more features for editing than the TikTok editor has, including trending videos and templates.

Always have a list

In your pocket or on your phone, I want you to always have a list of 20 video ideas for your business.

The pain with creating TikTok videos is not the filming of the video, it's the idea generation. Many of us will have a spare 15 minutes in our day and we will say to ourselves, 'I'm going to create a TikTok video'. But then we sit down, look at our phones, look around, look at our phones again, do some research, look at other accounts, get a snack, sit down and realise that it's been 15 minutes, and we still don't have any idea of what to create.

If you try and think of an idea and create the video at the same time, you will waste a lot of time and probably lose a lot of motivation. However, if you allocate time to only coming up with ideas and then allocate another time block for creating those videos, you will be much more efficient and happy with the outcome.

Let's talk about the list you need to make.

Start by writing down all the ideas you have and be detail focused. For example, one of them might be you packing orders with a voiceover. Write that idea down but don't leave it at that — take note of what sound you would like to use, what story you'll be telling with the voiceover and how long you want the video to be. The difference between your TikTok list and everyone else's is the detail.

Tip

Use tools to help you come up with ideas.

♦ TikTok search functionality: TikTok has one of the best search functionalities for social platforms. Search for a topic that you want to create a video about, and then use the filters to show the 'most liked' within the last week or month.

♦ Artificial intelligence (AI) tools such as ChatGPT: There are many AI tools that you can use — the main thing to work on is the type and quality of prompts that you give it. Be specific with what kind of hook you want and ask it to give you interesting facts.

♦ TikTok Creative Center: This is my favourite tool because it gives you trends, video topics and creators in that space.

Film B-roll content (and make it a habit)

The term 'B-roll' comes from filmmaking and is the foundation for great storytelling because it provides context to your story. In the making of films, there are two rolls of film: the A-roll and the B-roll. A-roll is the main footage — the hero shot. An example would be the lead actor delivering a monologue or having a conversation with the supporting characters.

B-roll is the second roll of film. This is the supplementary footage that adds depth and context to the A-roll. Think of scenes such as the bustling streets of New York, snow falling on the ground or tree branches swaying in the wind. B-roll clips are used to cut away from the main action to not only provide more context, but to make the scene more interesting.

HOW DOES THIS APPLY TO TIKTOK?

Imagine you're discussing your new product. While you talk, you can add in B-roll of the product in action — perhaps a customer unboxing it or you trying it on. This breaks the monotony of one type of visual. Remember, TikTok thrives on fast-paced and highly engaging storytelling. Attention spans are short, so this is a great way to keep them hooked.

HOW DO YOU DO IT?

B-roll clips include you filming a few seconds of all your activities throughout the day. You can either place the camera on a stand and film yourself doing the activity or you can simply film what's around you. Here are some examples:

- making your coffee

- walking the dog

- writing emails

- doing your makeup

- having a meeting

- packing an order

- talking to your team

- buying office supplies.

The challenge is remembering to film the content. I actually put reminders in my calendar so that I film key things in my day. It needs to become a habit.

The reason you want to have B-roll clips in your camera roll is because it makes creating content ten times easier. I'm going to show you the different ways you can use this sort of content.

- Voiceover: Use clips from your day to make a 15- to 30-second video and do a voiceover talking about what happened in your day.

- Green screen: Use a few clips and then use the green screen filter to talk about something weird or exciting that happened.

- Trending sound: Create a short video (seven to ten seconds) with some B-roll clips and use a trending sound.

Think of ONE story to share per day

If there is one video you can create every day, it's a story about something that happened to you. Big or small, it doesn't matter. What matters is how you tell it.

When creating this type of content, there needs to be a hook, some context, the climax and the resolution. So regardless of the story itself, you still need to have all of these elements to create a good piece of content. People always think they need a big story, but sometimes the simplest of stories can be incredibly engaging.

Here are some ideas:

- something you overheard
- someone was rude to you
- you received a negative review
- you saw a customer place a repeat order with you
- you received a lovely or not-so-lovely email
- your kid said something profound.

For this, you can use B-roll clips or speak directly to the camera.

Use the BE SEEN framework

BE SEEN is the best way to come up with content ideas for your business. I created this to help me with my content strategy, and it has helped me generate millions of views.

We are going to use BE SEEN as a content pillar — different topic areas that you should frequently create content around:

◆ Behind the scenes

◆ Enemy

◆ Storytelling

◆ Expertise

◆ Experience

◆ Newsjacking

Behind the scenes (BTS)

BTS content showcases the reality of your business: how you pack products, what the office looks like, what you eat for lunch, who your team members are and so on. BTS content gives context to your storytelling and creates a three-dimensional view of your business. This is incredibly engaging for your customers and audience to see.

Enemy

This is something that cult brands do exceptionally well — they create an enemy to fight against. This could be a person, thing or concept; for example, Patagonia fights against the 'dirty denim' industry and promotes ethical manufacturing. These sorts of videos create a cult-like following because it allows people with similar values to find you. We cover this in more detail in Chapter 31.

Storytelling

This is the human side of your business and is really about your story as the founder. You can talk about your business journey, mistakes, aspirations and key events in your life. Focus on creating an emotional response.

Expertise

These are the tips and the educational things that you know more about than anyone else in your industry. This is a great place to showcase your authority.

Experience

These videos are more to do with the products or services that you sell, but rather than just talking about the product features and benefits, focus on the experience that customers have when they shop with you. You can talk about their pain points and how you solve them, and you can also talk about how you surprise and delight them with every order. These sorts of videos can include unboxings and user-generated content.

Newsjacking

This is a great way to get more views quickly. Newsjacking involves creating content around a trending topic, news story, celebrity news or something that everyone is talking about. The idea is to give your opinion on the news and relate it back to your product or industry. One of my tips, which is optional, is to be polarising with your opinion. You don't necessarily need to put a negative spin on it, but you can talk about a point of view that many people may not agree with. The combination of a trending topic and a polarising opinion makes for an incredibly viral-worthy video.

An example of this is when I created a video about Mikayla Nogueira (a famous TikToker). At the time, she was trending because she had created a paid video for a L'Oreal mascara. Other creators on TikTok were calling her out for allegedly faking the mascara results by adding false lashes. It was a polarising topic and hundreds of creators were talking about it online. I created a video about L'Oreal's creative marketing strategy behind the video. I was able to weave in a trending topic with my marketing knowledge to create an educational and entertaining video for my audience. The video received 168 000 views and over 4000 likes.

Many brands use newsjacking to quickly reach thousands of new people. The key is to always keep an eye out for topics that are trending that can be related to your product or service and to quickly act on it.

Q&A with Brittney Saunders, founder of Fayt The Label

Brittney Saunders is an incredibly successful founder on TikTok. Over ten years ago, she ventured into the world of YouTube before the word 'influencer' even existed. Brittney amassed over 1 million followers in her late teens and early twenties, mastering the art of captivating an audience and creating a personal brand that would, ultimately, serve as the launchpad for her thriving fashion label, Fayt The Label.

In the last couple of years, both Brittney and Fayt have created some of the most viral and hilarious videos on TikTok, propelling her brand awareness to new heights. She is one of the few people who truly understands how content marketing and brand awareness can grow a business. I interviewed her so I could really understand how she reaches new audiences every single day.

Your first few videos on TikTok got between 2000 and 5000 views. Coming from over one million subscribers on YouTube and hundreds of thousands of views on your videos, did the TikTok numbers bother you?

No, not at all! I've never actually given a crap about the actual numbers to the point where I have cared if something performed great and something performed crap in comparison. I always know, especially when we are starting out something on a new app, that the results are going to be lower. We still even try

TikTok trends every week to this day, and some do great and others don't — it doesn't matter. It's the fact that you're giving it a go that matters the most.

The first viral TikTok video (80k views) was a video of you posing in one of Fayt's best-selling tops with your voiceover talking about the benefits of the top. Do you think there is always a direct correlation between a founder showing their face and the engagement on those videos?

Definitely. It adds such a personal element to a brand and business. It gives the customer another reason to like a brand because there's someone in their face that they can potentially like or relate to; it's not just a product, but a person.

Your more recent videos for Fayt The Label are more candid, funny and not in Fayt's usual branding, which was focused on aesthetics. Can you tell me about the transition to more raw content?

The internet and social apps have definitely changed a lot since we first made our TikTok account. Back then it really was all about the pretty videos and models posing, but over the last few years, that hasn't really worked anymore. We still make this type of content but have found that making real, relatable and raw content just adds such a personal element to our brand, and if I'm being honest, it's more 'me'. I am far from 'aesthetic' in my own life. I'm honestly a Newy [Newcastle] bogan, so going out of my way to make perfectly curated videos is not who I am at all.

Your most viral videos are when you are talking to the camera. Why don't you do that for all your videos? What is the importance of having different types of content?

I guess we don't make every video that way, because it would very quickly become repetitive, and people would probably get sick of it. It's important to identify which types of content work best for your business and audience — like us with the videos of me talking to the camera, but also being mindful of needing to serve your audience with other types of content as well. After all, Fayt isn't just me.

Do you create videos for TikTok and then repurpose them for Instagram? Or the other way around?

Yes! I know a lot of people say to only ever make certain content for Instagram or only make certain types of content for TikTok, but we make it for both! Sometimes one piece of content will flop on Instagram but then perform amazingly on TikTok, sometimes one piece of content will blow up on both apps! I say go for it and use your content across both platforms.

So much of your content (dancing around the warehouse, lip synching trending sounds, talking to the camera) is a true reflection of your personality—what is your advice to business owners who may be too shy to create similar content?

I totally get it, not everyone wants to be on camera. Some people don't want to show their face or don't feel confident talking on camera. I think it's all about finding what it is that *you can do* and honing in on that.

How much time do you allocate every day for content creation?

Less than ten minutes! Making TikToks takes no time at all, especially the funny/silly videos! You can allocate ten minutes of your day to making a 30-second video easily. People always say it's hard, but it really isn't—but again, maybe this falls back on me and how much experience I have.

What type of video results in the biggest number of orders/sales?

Hmm. . . it's really hard to say. If I had to define it, I'd say the videos that result in the most sales are the videos that come across as the least 'salesy'. The more organic the video, the better.

If you started a new brand from scratch, knowing what you know now about TikTok, what videos would you would create?

I'd make videos from day one, me sitting in whatever room I'm in at home and I'd talk to the camera saying 'I'm starting a _____ business and I'm going to take you along with me every step of the way'. I'd use TikTok like it was my own personal video journal/ diary, well before the products even came into play. I'd try to build a community that would become invested in the journey of me starting up my own business.

What advice do you always find yourself giving to other business owners?

I think the number one thing people always come to me for is just that boost of encouragement and a push in the right direction. I find most people are held back by their own worries and 'what ifs' or just that general fear of failure. I truly believe that your journey to success begins on the other side of that fear or that huge risk, or even that tough conversation. One of my mottos that I live by is 'hard conversations, easy life, easy conversations, hard life'.

CHAPTER 11

TOFU strategy #6: TikTok ads

If you want brand awareness, TikTok ads will give it to you. TikTok has been built purely as a brand-awareness platform, and while its organic platform does a pretty good job, its paid ads platform does an incredible job.

One of the best strategies I've seen businesses use to boost their brand visibility is to pay for followers on TikTok via paid ads. There are a few benefits to this. You can:

- increase your follower count by the thousands for less than $100

- automatically get better engagement because you have targeted specific followers

- unlock key features on TikTok as your follower count grows, such as adding a link to your bio.

So if you haven't already, the first step is to set up a TikTok ads account in TikTok Ads Manager and link your TikTok account.

10x your followers and engagement

That wasn't a click bait heading! Using TikTok ads is a great way to get more followers and boost brand engagement. Brands have literally been built on the back of exponentially growing their followers on TikTok using paid ads. Regardless of your budget, testing paid TikTok ads is a must for your business.

Let's talk about how to create a TOFU TikTok ad. You need to keep in mind that ad platforms always change; therefore, I'll keep these steps as broad as possible so you can follow along at any time. The strategy behind creating these ads does not change.

In any ad campaign, whether it's Meta, Google or TikTok, the campaign always has three main parts: the objective and budget, the audience selection, and the ad creative/copy. So, similar to Meta ads, which we've already covered in Chapter 6, we'll be looking at the same areas for TikTok ads.

Objective

For this particular TikTok ad, to get more followers, the objective will be 'community interaction'. That title may change over time, but at the core, TikTok will always specify what objectives you can expect to achieve. You want to choose the objective that gets you more followers.

Budget

For your budget, I suggest starting with $30 per day. This is my go-to campaign budget for any new paid ad that I test. TikTok recommends a $50 per day spend on any campaign. This is to help TikTok optimise the ad much faster, but it's not necessary when you are just starting. If your business has additional marketing funds to spend, then you can certainly increase this budget to kick off the ad.

Audience

As TikTok becomes more and more mature as a platform, its audience selection will become more sophisticated, and you will be able to be more specific in your targeting. Currently, TikTok allows you to choose demographics (like country, gender and age) and interests. A really cool feature is the ability to also select people who follow creators in certain categories and people who interact with certain hashtags. When launching TOFU ads for the first time, I like to keep the audience selection more broad before narrowing it down.

Optimisation goal

This tells TikTok what you want to achieve. The best option is to select 'Follow' to optimise for more followers. Once you have picked your audience and optimisation goal, you can move to the ad creation stage.

Ad creation

Here, you can choose a TikTok video you have already posted, or you can upload a new video. It's always better to choose a video you have already posted that has performed well organically. This is because it's more likely to get engagement when you put ad spend behind it. Using an existing video also allows TikTok to optimise your ad faster because it already has existing organic data for the video.

Similar to Meta ads, you can choose multiple videos to promote. I highly recommend you test at least three videos because you will get a good indication of what type of content that audience engages with more.

Tip

You can choose to run a TikTok ad through TikTok Ads Manager or you can simply promote a video through your TikTok mobile app, similar to boosting Instagram posts, which has been around for years. But it is always best to use the ads manager as you have a lot more control over the audience and the objective. However, if you just want to try TikTok ads in a quick and easy way, then try promoting a video on the app. This might get you good results and motivate you to go more in-depth in the ads manager.

CHAPTER 12

TOFU strategy #7: Instagram

Ah, Instagram. I have a particular soft spot for Instagram because this is the platform I used to build my social following for Hero Packaging, and our community of Heroes has mainly grown on Instagram. Fast forward to today and Hero Packaging has over 99000 followers on Instagram who are highly engaged business owners who care for the planet. I have always been able to rely on this engaged community to drive website traffic and fill the TOFU. Building this following has also given me a very intimate understanding of Instagram as an organic social media platform.

Over time, I have found that the main problem with Instagram is discoverability. Traditionally, Instagram was used as a true social and community network, where your content would be shown only to your audience (people who already follow you). It was difficult to grow through organic content creation. The only ways to be seen by new people were when an account with many followers tagged you or your content was shared.

Recently, Instagram has started changing. With the introduction of TikTok, where discoverability is the name of the game, Instagram is also focusing on account discoverability.

I predict that this will become an even bigger focus for Instagram in the next couple of years as it competes with TikTok. This is a great thing for businesses because they can once again start using Instagram organically to genuinely reach new people and not just their existing followers.

So, how do you target a cold audience (in your TOFU) on Instagram? Right now, it's about short form content, specifically reels. But tomorrow, the algorithm may favour photos again and in six months there may be a new form of media that it prefers.

So, I'm not going to teach you how to create a reel or a post. That knowledge will only be useful for a short amount of time, and there are also many helpful resources online. Instead, I'm going to tell you how to always stay ahead of the curve and create content that attracts a new audience, regardless of how the Instagram algorithm changes over time. Here are three things you should always do:

1. follow Instagram experts

2. watch the trends

3. focus on high-quality content.

1. Follow Instagram experts

Instagram releases updates frequently and rewards brands and creators who jump on them quickly. Your job is to find creators who are at the forefront of Instagram updates. An example is Adam Mosseri, the head of Instagram. He is always going to be the first person who talks about an Instagram update.

Now, I want you to search on Instagram for 'Instagram expert' and 'Instagram growth coach' and look through the results for people who are at the forefront of Instagram strategies. Follow them and start creating content based on their advice.

2. Watch the trends

The easiest way to grow on Instagram is following the trends. Following creators who are up-to-date with trends is a great way to ride any trend wave. You can also just browse Instagram and TikTok and take note of sounds or styles of videos that keep coming up.

No matter what the trend is, you can make your own version of it. A year ago, lip synching and dancing and pointing to text was all the rage. I was never comfortable doing any of that, so I just used the trending sound as a quiet music overlay while I spoke to the camera. Those videos had great reach and I didn't have to do something I didn't want to do.

My advice is to use trending elements, such as a trending sound or style, but create it in a way that's authentic to your brand personality.

3. Focus on high-quality content (obviously!)

High-quality content isn't what you think. It's definitely not studio-quality content or a gorgeous photo shoot with models. When I talk about high quality, I am referring to content that is useful, entertaining and highly engaging.

As a business owner, much of the content we produce is to sell our products, and that's okay. But you're most likely getting a few likes here and there, none of which are from a cold audience and none of which are resulting in sales. The way content works is that when you post it, it gets shown to a small group of people first (based on the keywords and hashtags you use), and based on how those people engage with it (watch time, saves, comments, likes), Instagram will choose whether or not to push it out to a slightly larger group of people. If it continues to perform well, it will continue pushing it out to a larger group of people and then again to more people. But if the content doesn't perform well, the reach simply stops.

As I said before, I have used Instagram a lot to grow Hero Packaging, and creating engaging content has always been a sure-fire way to ensure my posts perform well. So, here's what I want you to do. You are going to focus on these four things when you create content:

1. useful industry knowledge

2. storytelling

3. product tips, hacks, secret features

4. a current news story or pop-culture event.

Useful industry knowledge

I bet you have a seriously good inside scoop on your industry.

If you're in the jewellery industry, do you know the cheap tricks that other brands use to make their jewellery look expensive? Are there certain metals that people should avoid? Why is gold so much more expensive than silver?

If you're in the candle industry, do you know why some candles burn longer than others? What percentage of candles are bought by men and what scent do they buy? What scents can help with anxiety?

If you're in the fashion space, what is a huge myth that isn't true in your industry? Do clothes actually cost more to manufacture in different sizes? Can you explain exactly what polyester is and how it's made? Where do most of the materials come from?

You get the idea. Talking about your 'insider' industry knowledge is not only extremely interesting, but also makes you an authority figure in that space.

It's also shareable and that's another metric that will guarantee more eyeballs on your content.

Storytelling

Once upon a time, a girl called Anaita created content about a new product offering in her business. She posted this content to her brand's Instagram account, and within a week, she had 13 000 of her own followers and 415 000 non-followers view her content, and she gained over 8000 brand new followers. She was so happy. Anaita and her new followers lived happily ever after.

There is absolutely no better content than storytelling content. I don't care how the algorithm changes or what is trending, storytelling content is evergreen and will always perform better than most of your other content. That's because it's personal and is centred around emotion.

Tip

You are creating content for a cold audience, which means they have never heard about you or seen you before. So, the storytelling content has to be standalone content. Don't assume that the viewers know about your life or business. The key to a great TOFU video is a main event or plot around which everything is centred. Hooks (the first three seconds of the video) play a huge part in this.

For example, if I'm talking about my day in the life of a business owner I could either start the video like this: 'This is a day in my life as a business owner.'

Or like this: 'I just got a two-star review and I need your help. Let me start from the beginning…'

The latter is much more entertaining because it is focused on one key plot.

There are many types of storytelling content, but the two types that work the best are live stories and past experiences. Both include BTS and inside-the-business content.

FACETIME CHAT

A great creator of FaceTime content is Anna Paul. All of her content is storytelling content, but she frames it in a way that makes you feel like it's happening right now. She's telling you about her day in a FaceTime format like you're her best friend. She centres the whole video around one key event in her day, but shows you everything that happened in the lead-up to that event.

Another great creator of live stories is Bridey Drake. She makes you feel like she's talking directly to you. She does this by talking to the camera in a conversational way and telling you about something that she is currently doing. She takes you along with her while she does daily tasks, such as going to the post office or driving to the beach for a morning swim. Her content makes you feel like you are experiencing it all in real time.

Both of these creators also have brands, and they use the same storytelling technique for those brands.

FaceTime chats are engaging because they bring the audience into your world. They are easy to create because you film B-roll content (see page 88 for a refresher) and piece it together at the end of the day with a voiceover narrating the day.

Here are some ideas to create FaceTime chat in your content:

◆ A day in your life as a business owner, focusing on one thing that happened to you.

◆ Something that your team member said that affected your entire day.

◆ A crazy thing you decided to do today.

◆ Packing orders while talking about what you're going through or feeling.

PAST EXPERIENCES

Past experiences means telling a story about something that happened to you a while ago and sharing what you learnt from it or how it has affected you. These are usually done in an inspirational way.

For example, in many of my Instagram videos, I talk about business lessons my mum taught me when she started her own medical practice 20 years ago. These lessons have shaped me as a business owner today.

Similarly, you would have hundreds of past experiences that you can talk about for your business. The important thing is to relate it to your business in some way. The best kind of videos are when you can take a negative and turn it into something inspirational or aspirational. Examples include:

◆ When someone said something negative to you and you turned it into a positive.

◆ When clothing didn't fit right on you, so you created it yourself.

◆ When you used to be disorganised and couldn't find a system that worked, so you created a productivity journal.

Again, remember the goal of this content is attracting new eyeballs, so the punchier the story, the more Instagram will push the reach of the content.

Product tips, hacks, secret features

Product hacks are a great way to get in front of a new audience.

When you talk about simple product benefits, Instagram knows that a new audience won't really be interested in that. However, a product hack that is a little bit shocking or surprising has universal appeal, and has a big chance of getting shown to a cold audience.

Who Gives A Crap, the sustainable toilet paper company, does this really well. Here are some examples:

◆ Using the toilet paper covering as gift-wrapping for Valentine's Day.

◆ Using stacked toilet paper rolls to make a Christmas Tree.

◆ Using bums to make pottery (their whole business is related to butt jokes).

Product hack videos or photos should be short and sharp and have a surprise element. Let's go through some examples that will give you inspiration:

◆ A swimsuit that can be transformed into a top for a date to a fancy restaurant.

◆ A secret pocket in a jacket to store a beer.

- Wet wipes that double as sweat wipes.

- Exercise tights that can be worn straight from gym to work — how to style it.

- A fragrance that secretly repels mosquitoes.

- A pair of earrings that makes you look wealthy.

- A hair curler that can give you Hailey Bieber's hairstyle.

Get that creative brain thinking.

Current news story or pop-culture event

This is one of my favourite Instagram tactics to reach a cold audience.

If you talk about trending news or celebrity happenings, anyone who is interested in that topic (followers and non-followers) will be shown your content. Here is how to do it:

- Scan news headlines to see what is being talked about (refrain from anything too negative).

- Scan TikTok to see if anything interesting is currently happening in pop culture.

- Look at celebrity accounts to see what they are talking about.

- Find links between what you find and your industry or product.

- Give your opinion on the news or add facts and details that no one else knows.

Tip

In order for Instagram to pick up the news story or event you are talking about, make sure to utilise Instagram SEO. Use the news headlines in your caption and text overlay. You can also use related hashtags.

STAGE 2

Warming up the audience in the MOFU

Type of audience: Warm
Your goal: Website traffic

So far we've gone through marketing strategies to fill the top of your marketing funnel. The TOFU was focused on cold audiences and getting your brand in front of people who have never heard of you. Now your job is to push these people further down the funnel and start warming them up so they're closer to making a purchase.

Let me ask you a question: how many of your Instagram followers do you think have bought from your business? 75 per cent? 50 per cent? 30 per cent?

What if I told you that, on average, less than 10 per cent of your followers are your customers? In many cases, less than 5 per cent of a brand's followers turn into paying customers.

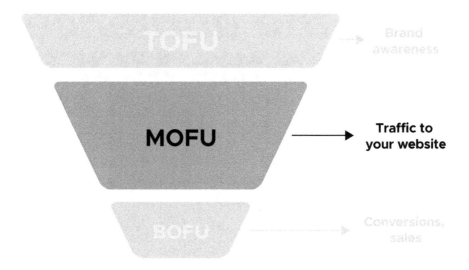

TOFU — Brand awareness

MOFU ⟶ **Traffic to your website**

BOFU — Conversions, sales

This is quite a frustrating statistic because it shows that followers may just be a vanity metric. If you can't convert them to a sale, do they even matter?

This is similar to website visitors. If the average conversion rate is less than 2 per cent, then do 98 per cent of your website visitors even matter?

The answer is yes! They matter because they provide a huge opportunity for you. These mid-funnel followers and website visitors have shown an interest in your brand and may already love what you do. They simply have not been convinced to add anything to cart or make a purchase. So, let's talk about the best strategies to get them to do exactly that.

MOFU

CHAPTER 13

MOFU strategy #1: Meta ads

I want to tell you about a big mistake I made in my business. There was one month in Hero Packaging where I had looked at our profit-and-loss statement and saw that we were spending way too much on marketing, so on an impulse, I stopped all our Meta ads. I thought that if I could bring people to the website in other (cheaper) ways, then I would save us $30000 per month. However, within 24 hours of stopping the ads, our website traffic decreased by 50 per cent. The slowdown in traffic also meant a slowdown in sales. It was scary to see. I tried other ways to bring more people to the website, but when traffic didn't increase, I knew I had made a huge mistake.

I know that we should never rely on one platform to generate all of our website traffic — we should have a multi-channel approach, including email marketing, social media and SEO. However, the difference with Meta ads compared with the other strategies is that it sends a consistent stream of traffic to your site.

That's why it is the first strategy I want to talk to you about. As we've already covered the basics of Meta ads in our TOFU strategies, I'm going to get straight into the nitty gritty. For your warm audience, there is only one campaign you need to set up.

Meta ads MOFU strategy

Objective: Sales/conversions.

Type of campaign: Manual.

Budget: A great starting budget is $20 per day, but change this to what your marketing budget allows.

Audience: In the MOFU, you want to target a very specific audience. These are people who have:

◆ engaged with one of your ads

◆ engaged with you on Facebook or Instagram

◆ visited your website.

But who have *not*:

◆ added anything to their cart.

Simply put, this is your warm audience: people who have heard about you, but haven't considered buying from you yet.

In order to target them, you need to create these audiences in the 'Audience' tab in your Meta ads. Ad platforms will chop and change over time, but the strategy behind the ads will remain the same. Therefore, I'll be going through the types of audiences you need to set up, but not the step-by-step instructions (you can always find additional help for this online if needed). So, let's continue and create the following audiences:

- website visitors in the last 180 days

- people who have engaged with your brand on Instagram in the last 365 days

- people who have engaged with your brand on Facebook in the last 365 days

- people who have added to cart in the last 180 days (you will be excluding this audience).

Ad creative: When creating ad creatives for this campaign, you have to remember that the people seeing these ads have some kind of familiarity with your brand, so the ads should convince them to take action by clicking on the ad to browse your products, learn about your story or get details about a particular product.

Here are some great examples of ad creatives you can use in your MOFU ads:

- Founder video: Talk about why you started this business and your purpose.

- BTS: Give people a sneak peek into how you run the business or what your warehouse/packing station looks like.

- Packing orders: Use a voiceover while you pack your orders and talk about your products.

- Lifestyle videos: Choose a video of your product in use. This could be a user-generated video or a video of you demonstrating how to use it. The more popular your product seems to be, the higher the incentive to click through to your website.

◆ Review videos: Pick a glowing review and use it as the basis of your video.

Copy: The copy should acknowledge that the audience has heard about your brand or product. Here are some examples of copy you could use:

◆ Have you wanted to try this?

◆ Over 1000 people have given this five stars

◆ It's time to finally check out the....

◆ Want to learn more about...?

◆ Join us in our mission to...

◆ I think you'll love this

◆ OK, so you've heard of us, but I bet you didn't know we...

Your MOFU Meta campaign has been set up! Excellent! As always, you need to monitor, test and update your campaigns over time to continually optimise them. But by simply launching this type of Meta ad, you should see an increase in website traffic and sales. If the campaign appears to be performing well, try increasing the budget gradually in 20 per cent increments and see if your sales continue to grow.

CHAPTER 14

MOFU strategy #2: Email marketing

While Meta ads may drive consistent website traffic, there is nothing quite as exciting as getting an influx of visitors from a free email. Some of the largest e-commerce companies in the world derive 30 per cent of their daily website traffic from their email marketing. This is huge!

I know I don't need to tell you how valuable email marketing is, but here are three things I bet you don't know about the power of emails:

1. It has a 36x return on investment (ROI): for every dollar spent on your email platform, you get $36 back on average (as reported by Hubspot).

2. Emails can generate more money than Facebook ads and Google ads to the same targeted audience.

3. It is so powerful for some companies that 37 per cent of direct-to-customer businesses send emails every single day.

When you send an email to your subscribers, it's difficult to measure its success without a benchmark. It's important to not only analyse your own results, but also look at other businesses to see how your emails perform in comparison. According to Hubspot (2023), here are some email stats that are a good starting point when assessing your email success. The average:

- open rate for emails is 21.5 per cent

- click-through rate is 2.3 per cent

- unsubscribe rate is 0.1 per cent.

So, if you send an email to 1000 people, on average, 215 people will open the email, and 23 people will click through. And only one person will unsubscribe.

'But I don't want them to unsubscribe'

When I speak to business owners, one of the most common things I hear is: 'I don't want people to unsubscribe.' I always say: 'Let them go. We don't want them anyway.'

Regardless of what you think, people who unsubscribe were always going to unsubscribe. They weren't interested in getting your marketing emails — they either signed up to get a discount code or accidently signed up when checking out. It is not your email that made them leave; it was simply a reminder for them to do so.

Let me tell you a secret: when people unsubscribe, it makes your database perform better for your business. It leads to higher open rates and click-through rates. It also helps with deliverability (less risk of your emails landing in customers' spam folders).

So, as sad as it is to see that number next to the 'unsubscribes' in your email metrics, remember that your emails will perform better because of it.

Email strategy part 1: How to get subscribers

In my ten years of business, getting email subscribers has always been one of the most challenging things to do. For many business owners, having a popup on their website has been the only way they have gathered email addresses, but consumers are quick to shut down popups as soon as they appear, resulting in less than 10 per cent of website visitors signing up.

I've been fortunate to speak to hundreds of business owners and have seen some email collection strategies that work. Let's go through them:

- the dreaded popup

- Instagram story promotions

- run a giveaway

- brand collaboration

- use a lead magnet.

The dreaded popup

Should I have a popup? Or should I not have a popup? It's an age-old question, and the winning response has always been: you should have a popup.

Popups are a great way to capture some of the visitors that hit your website every day. Yes, they're annoying. Yes, they always pop up at the wrong time. Yes, they always have a pretty low-ball offer. But they work.

Here is what I recommend when it comes to popups:

- Don't make it load as soon as someone lands on your site. Give them time to have a look around. Loading a popup after 30 seconds is much better than having it pop up before that visitor even knows what you sell.

- To capture people leaving, you can test having an exit-intent popup instead. So, if it looks like they are about to leave, a popup will be triggered with copy that may say: 'Before you go, here's 15 per cent off.'

- Keep it simple. The fields should be first name and email address. Anything more than that, and you'll see a huge drop in sign ups.

- Test different offers every two weeks and compare the difference. Test 10 per cent off, 15 per cent off, $10 off, $12 off, free shipping or any other offer you can think of.

- Make sure it's easy to close the popup. Sometimes the 'x' or 'close' button is hidden, and this makes for a terrible user experience.

Instagram story promotions

If you have pretty good Instagram engagement, then encouraging signups through Instagram stories is a strong tactic.

The reason I prefer stories over posts is because it's a one click or one swipe action to get people to your site. If you create a reel or a post, your audience needs to go to your bio, click the link, and then click the right link on your Linktree page. It's way too much effort and it won't be as successful.

To use this tactic successfully, here are some things you should do:

- Make your audience excited about something: it could be a new product launch, a restock or a sale.

- Make it known that subscribers will be the first to have access to it.

- Talk about it in your stories and on each story have a link to your sign-up page.

Run a giveaway

This is the e-commerce email sign-up hack successful brands are doing that we all need to copy. The idea is to have a constant giveaway running. For example, you can have an ongoing competition where one person wins a product, a sum of money or store credit every week.

The trick is to run a Meta ad for this giveaway. The ad will run to your MOFU audience (a warm audience) or to a broader audience if your product has broad appeal, and they click through to a sign-up page to enter the competition.

Every week or month, you select a random winner and make an announcement on social media.

There are some brands I know who spend about $6000 per month on giveaway ads because they generate over 10000 sign ups each month.

When you run an ad, the ideal cost per sign up is between $0.60 and $2.

MOFU

Brand collaboration

As mentioned in Chapter 9, a brand collaboration is when two or more brands join forces to create a new product, promote a product or do a giveaway. It's usually a strategy where each brand will contribute a product or service of equal value. For the purposes of gaining more email subscribers, brand collaborations leverage each business's database to grow their own.

One of the best examples of this was when Three Birds Renovations collaborated with TileCloud. The two businesses created a collection of tiles and ran a giveaway. Three Birds Renovations emailed their database asking their audience to fill in their details (including their email address) on TileCloud's website. Tile Cloud received over 100 000 new email sign ups in this campaign. All the people who signed up were in their target market. In return, TileCloud provided tiles for the renovations that Three Birds were working on, and created collections on its website that showcased the tiles used in those homes.

On a smaller scale, two small businesses I coached collaborated with each other on a giveaway. They decided to 'swap' SMS subscribers instead of email subscribers. They did a cross-promotion and split the cost of a Facebook ad over four days. They both received nearly 2500 new SMS subscribers.

If you want to do a brand collaboration to get new email subscribers, this is one way to do it:

◆ You select a brand to collaborate with. They should have a similar-sized email database to yours, with a very similar target audience.

◆ You both decide on the collaboration offering. It could be that you do a giveaway together or create a bundle/product together.

◆ You select a date to launch it.

◆ On that date and time, you both send an email to your subscribers with the offer. In order to get the offer, your audience will sign up to their database on their site and their audience will sign up to your database on your website.

An alternative method is to pay the brand to talk about your brand in their emails and to have a link to your sign-up page. Essentially you 'swap' your email addresses for theirs or you pay for theirs.

Tip

When choosing a partner brand, make sure:

◆ they aren't your competitor, and they don't have the potential to become your competitor in the future

◆ their email list is a similar size to yours: ask for their analytics, such as open rate and click-through rate for their engaged subscribers

◆ a contract is signed by both or all businesses that covers the deliverables and responsibilities for all parties.

Use a lead magnet

Have you ever seen an article pop up on your Facebook feed titled something like, 'These are the three most effective ways to fall asleep according to experts' or 'Here's a free e-book designed to help you lose weight within 14 days'? When you click on those articles, it takes you to a landing page where you enter your email address to get the article, e-book, guide or course sent to you. This is a lead magnet.

Simply put, a lead magnet is information in the form of a report, newsletter, white paper, e-book, guide or sample that your target market would love to know or receive.

Traditionally, lead magnets have been used by service-based businesses, but they can also be a huge generator of e-commerce leads if done well. Let's go through some lead magnets in different categories:

◆ E-book: How to apply lashes like a technician.

◆ Guide: Ten top tips for your third trimester.

◆ Template: A fitness template to gain muscle in 28 days.

◆ Quiz: What skin type are you?

◆ Report: How clean is the tap water in your area?

How to implement it in your email collection strategy:

◆ Use frequently asked questions from your customers or use a website, such as Answer the Public or Trending Topics, to find a topic that is very popular amongst your target market.

◆ Create a digital resource with useful information. I like to use Canva to create digital assets and I save them as a PDF.

◆ Head to your website platform. If you use Shopify, upload your PDF to your files, and copy and paste its URL into your notes. You will need this URL later.

◆ Use your email platform, such as Klaviyo, to create an audience list where those subscribers will sit. Name it something you can easily remember.

- ◆ Now, using your email platform, create an embedded form. This form should tell the consumer what the guide is about and include a field for their first name and email address. Link this form to the audience list you created above.

- ◆ Create a page on your website and embed the form there.

- ◆ Now create an email flow (more on this next). Make sure the trigger is when someone signs up to that new audience list, the email message will say something like, 'Thank you for signing up! Here is your free guide to [your topic].' Paste the URL that you copied from Shopify above.

Now it is up to you to promote that free downloadable. You can do this through Meta ads, social media or your website (as a popup or in the announcement bar).

One of the best examples of an e-commerce lead magnet was from Jolie Skin Co. Jolie Skin is an online retailer that sells shower heads and filters. They promote themselves as a haircare and skincare brand because using filtered water can improve consumers' hair and skin. They cleverly like to call it 'Step 0' in your beauty routine.

Jolie Skin created a downloadable water report that identifies the water toxicity in any suburb in the United States. When you click through to their sign-up landing page, it asks you for your zip/postcode and email address. It then emails you a postcode-specific water report that goes through all the toxic elements in your water supply.

This is such a fantastic way to collect email addresses and generate demand for their products because everyone wants to know how good or bad their water is. Jolie run this as an ongoing Facebook ad and even has it as a popup on their website. When they first created this downloadable report, they tripled their email subscribers in one month.

Now that you have put some email list growth strategies in place, it's time to send some actual email campaigns to get hundreds or thousands of people to your website.

Email strategy part 2: Email flows and email campaigns

Once you have started collecting email addresses, it's time to start communicating to those people. There are two types of ways to communicate with your subscribers: email flows and email campaigns. The main difference between them is automation — email flows are automatically sent when someone does or doesn't do something specific on your website, such as sign up to your list or purchase a product, while email campaigns are created manually, usually with an announcement, new product offering or sale.

Let's dive into strategies for both email flows and email campaigns.

Email flows

There aren't many marketing strategies that can generate revenue for your business 24/7, but automated email flows is one of the levers that work for you constantly without you needing to put in any extra effort. Whether you have automated emails going to ten people or 10 000 people, you don't work any harder. This makes email flows a huge part of growing your business.

Email flows, otherwise known as automations, are emails that are sent to your database automatically based on certain actions they've undertaken. For example, when someone adds something to their cart, an email is triggered to remind them to purchase. Or perhaps, if they signed up for a giveaway, an email is triggered to talk about how amazing your brand is.

The purpose of the email is to talk to the customer at the right point of their journey with you and encourage them to visit your website. Of course, a sale doesn't hurt either!

You know how we always hear marketers say you need to personalise the customer experience, and you have no idea what they're talking about because they never actually tell you? Well, email flows are part of personalisation marketing. They are triggered based on key actions, so it feels personalised for the recipient because the timing of the email is ideal for the customer. For example, if someone has signed up because they entered a giveaway, they will receive personalised emails about that giveaway. Or if someone signed up after making a purchase of one of your best-selling products, an email flow can give them more information about that specific product. Additionally, if you have asked for their first name when they signed up, you can use their name in the subject line and in emails.

According to research from Epsilon, 80 per cent of consumers are more likely to make a purchase when brands personalise the experience.

Here is a list of all the email flows your business should have set up (some of these are covered in later chapters):

- welcome series automations

- browse abandonment automations

- abandoned cart email automations (see Chapter 19)

- thank you email automations (see Chapter 22)

- product review automations (see Chapter 22)

- product replenishment (see Chapter 22)

MOFU

- back-in-stock automations (see Chapter 22)

- birthday automations (see Chapter 28).

Not all of these flows apply to MOFU marketing, so I'm going to take you through two MOFU email flows: welcome emails and browse abandonment emails. There are so many different email platforms available that change over time, so you can easily find step-by-step instructions on how to set up these email flows. I'm going to focus on the strategy and types of emails you need.

WELCOME SERIES EMAIL FLOW

The welcome series is like the first impression of your brand — it's the first bit of communication from your business to the subscriber. It begins as soon as someone signs up to your database for the first time.

Usually, the welcome series consists of three emails and introduces your products, highlights, all the aspects that makes your brand unique and tells your brand story. The series is 'triggered' with every new email subscriber, and they receive the following three emails.

EMAIL 1: THE FIRST WELCOME MESSAGE

Trigger: The trigger for the welcome series is when a person signs up to your email list. This could be via:

- a popup sign-up form on your website

- an embedded sign-up form on any landing page

- you manually adding a contact to your list.

The wait time: The first email in this series can be sent immediately. In virtually all instances, a subscriber's interest will never be higher than when they first sign up for your email list, so why wait to reach out to them?

The messaging: The first email is your chance to thank them for signing up, but it's also a great opportunity to tell them your brand or founder story: why you started this business and what your mission is. The email may even include a first-time purchase discount (if that's why they signed up in the first place).

Using a subject line that 'hooks' the reader is important! Here are some examples:

- Thank you, [name].

- Welcome to [your brand].

- I have to tell you this story.

- [Name], it's lovely to meet you.

- [Name], there's a surprise inside.

- Your discount code is inside.

Call to action: Don't miss any opportunity to get people to your website. You don't need to necessarily push them towards a sale, but you can get them to:

- learn more by clicking through to your 'About Us' page

- browse your homepage

- read a blog post

- learn about a product you highly recommend.

EMAIL 2: PROBLEM AND SOLUTION

Trigger: Someone signs up to your mailing list.

The wait time: Two days after they sign up (if no purchase has been made).

The messaging: Why did someone subscribe to your email list? It's usually because you offer something that solves some kind of problem. Your product may heal rosacea, it may give someone more self-confidence at the beach or it may be the perfect gift for a friend.

The second email in this series is to identify that problem and explain your solution. Here are some example problems from different categories:

◆ Have you never been able to find the perfect pair of jeans for your body type?

◆ Do you have adult acne that won't go away?

◆ Do you have that one person who is so difficult to buy for?

◆ Is it really hard to fall asleep at night?

◆ You want to grow your sales, but don't know where to start.

◆ Does your dog chew all your furniture?

◆ Do you want to enjoy the beach without worrying about what you look like?

Subject lines that work well for this email:

◆ We have solved it for you.

◆ Hate it when [problem]?

◆ Three ways you can improve [problem].

◆ You really need to see this.

Call to action: The CTA for this email is to push them towards a product or collection page as the solution to their problem.

EMAIL 3: PROOF OF HOW AMAZING YOU ARE (YOUR BUSINESS, THAT IS)

Trigger: Someone signs up to your mailing list.

The wait time: The second email in this series can be sent four days after they sign up (if no purchase has been made).

The messaging: This is the time to really prove to your customers that your products are amazing. You can do this in multiple ways:

- showcase before and afters

- include user-generated content

- include reviews about your products

- showcase any awards

- showcase a customer case study

- display all your best-selling products.

Call to action: In this email, you want to encourage them to click through to the product page and add to cart. You have prepped and primed them over the three emails, and now it's time for them to take action on your site.

BROWSE ABANDONMENT EMAIL FLOW

Imagine this: someone has seen your content on social media, clicked through to your website, signed up to your newsletter and browsed your products, but they leave before adding anything to their cart. We can assume that they liked what they saw on social media enough to click through to your website, but something has stopped them from adding to cart.

This is where a browse abandonment flow kicks in.

MOFU

In browse abandonment flows, a person does not have to add an item to their cart to trigger this flow — all they have to do is view an item and move on.

This email flow doesn't need to be complicated. We want to remind people of the products they saw and give them a little push to go back to the website and purchase.

Trigger: When someone views a product on your website but hasn't added it to their cart.

Wait time: One hour after browsing.

Messaging: This email will be specific to the product or products they were looking at. You can personalise the email with their name, and the main purpose is to remind them of those products. You can use copy like this for your subject lines and the body of the email:

- I saw you looking at me earlier.

- We noticed you noticing us.

- You have excellent taste.

- This would look great on you.

- Pick up where you left off.

- Shall I take you back to your new favourite product?

Call to action: The best CTA here is to direct them back to the product they were looking at. CTAs such as 'Take me back' or 'Shop my favourites' work really well here.

> **Tip**
>
> Keep your messaging simple. The customer has already shown interest in the item by looking at it on your website, so don't distract them with cross-selling or multiple CTAs.

EMAIL CAMPAIGNS

Email campaigns are the emails that you create and manually send out on a daily, weekly, monthly or ad-hoc basis. They are different to email flows because they are not automated based on triggers. Email campaigns have to be planned, created, written, designed and sent manually to your database.

I am notorious for signing up to email marketing, and so my personal inbox is flooded with marketing emails from everyone from tech companies to haircare businesses. I love to shop online, but I also love to spy on other brands and see what they send to their subscribers.

What I've noticed about different brands is the huge variation in their email marketing strategy. Some send emails every day, while some only send them when they have something to announce. Some brands use professional imagery while others use text-based emails or a lot more user-generated content.

As a consumer, I open marketing emails for a few different reasons:

- They are announcing something big.

- They have a sale running.

- They have restocked a product I was waiting for.

- The email is a note from the founder.

- There is something useful to learn.

As a consumer, I am selfish. I only want to see the emails that improve my life or when I can buy something on sale. This is what I want you to understand about your subscribers — they are selfish, so the emails should always include information that will benefit them.

Something I would like you to do is look through your previous email campaigns and take note of which emails received the highest open rate and click-through rate. Look at the subject lines and messaging of those emails to see what the people in your database love to read. This is a great place to start when thinking about what to send.

Here are some more email ideas for a warm audience:

◆ your brand story

◆ a note from the founder

◆ bestsellers

◆ social media; for example, 'Did we just become famous on TikTok?'

◆ things you didn't know about our products

◆ discounts and sales

◆ influencer collabs

◆ the collection that has sold out many times

◆ before and afters.

SHOULD I SEND THEM TO EVERYONE?

It is not best practice to send email campaigns to your full database every time you send an email. In fact, there are only a handful of times brands should be sending email campaigns to their full database. Those times are for big sales events, such as Black Friday, or big company announcements.

You should always try to segment your audiences and send emails that are valuable to them. This increases your email deliverability, open rate and click-through rate because your emails are more tailored to the people receiving them.

You can map this out as you go, and you can test different segments. One of my favourite email tactics is to send the same email to a few different segments to see which segment responds better.

Your database can be segmented by:

- products purchased

- date of purchase

- email interactions

- engagement level.

A common way to segment is by engagement level. Sending an email to an audience who is highly engaged will guarantee a much higher open rate and click-through rate. Continuously getting a high open rate and click-through rate helps your email deliverability for future emails.

Create an email newsletter

This is perhaps one of the best ways to do email campaigns. Creating a brand newsletter allows you to send emails without worrying about not having anything to say.

A newsletter is an email you send on a consistent basis (usually weekly or fortnightly) that has useful information about your industry.

For example, if you sell baby clothes, you can create a newsletter for parents of newborns. Each newsletter can have tips and guidance for each stage of their baby's life. It can also have trending parenting hacks and helpful products (yours included, of course).

A newsletter does not need to push your products, but they can be included organically in the email. The purpose of a newsletter is to show your knowledge in your industry and boost brand trust. The consistency and frequency of email newsletters is also beneficial for email deliverability — that means more of your emails will go to inboxes and not the junk folder.

Before we move on, it's important to just recap why your email marketing is so important in the MOFU. Some of the biggest global e-commerce companies derive a huge chunk of their daily website traffic from emails. As business owners, we work very hard to build our email databases. We'll not only put in a lot of our time, but also spend money on online ads to grow our subscribers. So, with all this hard work and money spent, it's critical to have a strong email marketing strategy to turn subscribers into paying customers.

CHAPTER 15

MOFU strategy #3: Google Ads

A single Google search ruined my love affair with my favourite skincare brand. I hadn't changed my cleanser brand in years. Every time I went to replenish my cleanser, I would type it into Google, click on that brand's website and buy the cleanser.

On one particular day, I typed the brand name into Google and I saw a new Google ad appear. It was for a brand I had heard about on TikTok, so I clicked on the ad to check out their cleansers. I loved the website and the ingredients they used, so I purchased not just the cleanser, but a serum and a moisturiser as well. I never went back to my original brand.

This is why I love Google Ads. It allows small businesses to gain visibility, even amongst bigger competitors.

However, for small businesses, Google Ads are often overlooked. The setup seems complex and the management of it seems overwhelming.

Many clients I've spoken to have said that it 'just looks too hard'. They decide to spend their money on Meta ads instead.

There are hundreds of business owners who haven't yet dived into Google Ads, and it's a big missed opportunity. Ideally, at any given point in time, you have Meta ads running *and* Google Ads running. These two paid tactics combined will make sure you have consistent brand awareness, website traffic and conversions in your business. It is not a case of one or the other: both work together to target as many people in your market as possible. The difference between Meta ads and Google Ads is intention.

When people see a Facebook ad, they are browsing on social media, laughing at a meme, liking their friend's posts or watching an entertaining video. They haven't gone to Facebook or Instagram to look for a solution to their problems.

But on search engines, people are only there to solve a problem — they have the intention to buy or learn — so showing up in front of them at a time when they need it most should lead to a much higher conversion rate.

The aim of this chapter is to tell you which Google Ads campaigns you should always have running, and explain how it all works.

We'll go through three types of Google Ads, and I will break down the different parts of the ad into:

- ◆ keywords (what keywords you should be targeting)

- ◆ headlines (the main copy of the ad)

- ◆ description (the copy underneath the headlines)

- ◆ sitelink extensions (the links underneath search ads).

Types of Google Ads

There are three types of Google Ads I want you to have in your business:

1. branded search ads

2. keyword-focused search ads

3. performance max (PMAX) ads.

Branded search ads

One of the cheapest and highest ROI search ads you can run as a business is a branded search campaign. As you gain more awareness and create more content, people will start Googling your brand name, and you want to make sure you own that space on Google.

In this campaign, you need to bid on your own brand name and multiple variations of it (sometimes including incorrect spelling!).

Whether you are just starting out, or have been in business for a while, creating a branded Google ad will allow people to find you easily and purchase from your store.

If your business is new, chances are your SEO hasn't started working yet, so by bidding on your brand name, you are capturing any person who is searching for it.

If you have been in business for a while, chances are your competitors are bidding on your brand name, so it's always best to have an ad to trump theirs. Another reason to bid on it is because people will hear about your brand from a number of sources, and one of the first things they will do is Google your name. It's important to own this online real estate.

MOFU

Let's look at an example. You own a business called Micah's Brushes, which sells detangling hairbrushes for kids.

Keywords: Target your brand name and any variations of your brand name, including spelling mistakes. Using the above example, you want to target keywords such as:

◆ Micah's Brushes

◆ Mica's brushes

◆ Myka's brushes

◆ Mycar hair brushes

◆ (you get the idea)

Headlines: Google gives you a few headlines, which it rotates until it finds the most optimised combination. The headline for branded search ads should always include your brand name, so pin that to the top. You can also add a brand tagline or a unique selling proposition (USP). Here are some options using the same example:

◆ Headline 1: Micah's Brushes (pinned)

◆ Headline 2: Best Detangling Brush for Kids

◆ Headline 3: Voted #1 by Aussie Parents

Description: Descriptions are there to give the user extra information about your business. You include information about your materials, ingredients, reviews and shipping.

Here are some options you could use for Micah's Brushes:

◆ Description 1: Soft bristles for a no-tears experience.

◆ Description 2: Over 400, five-star reviews.

- Description 3: Free shipping over $50.

- Description 4: Detangling hair doesn't need to be hard.

Sitelink extensions: These are the links under a Google ad that can lead a user to different parts of your website. You can lead them to best-selling products, your warranty page, your About Us page or an FAQs page.

Here are some examples:

- Best-selling blue brush

- Learn about how it works

- Read the reviews

- Money back guarantee

- Shop the Disney brush collection.

Keyword-focused search ads

For anyone who is searching for a product you sell or a problem that your brand solves, you need to have a Google ad that targets them. For example, if you sell weighted blankets, you may want to target keywords or keyword phrases such as:

- how to reduce anxiety

- heavy blankets

- anxiety blankets

- calming blankets.

By targeting these keywords on Google, you can capture anyone who is interested in what you sell.

It's important to think about keywords, and not just products. For example, let's say one of the products you sell is a microphone. Our first instinct is to create an ad that targets anyone who types 'microphone' into Google. It is, of course, a great place to start, but it's not the whole picture.

What you should be doing is thinking of what people are actually looking for when it comes to microphones. But how do you know what people are searching for? You use a free tool called 'Google Keyword Planner'.

Google Keyword Planner is one of the best free tools to find out what people are searching for, how many average searches there are per month and roughly what the cost per click is for those keywords. When you type in the keyword 'microphone' into Google Keyword Planner, it gives you related searches like:

- microphone for podcasting

- wireless microphone

- Rode microphone.

Knowing these related search terms is the best foundation for creating your keyword-based Google Ads. It's important to make a list of keywords and keyword phrases for each product or category in your store.

Let's create a Google keyword search ad based on the microphone example.

Keywords:

- Microphone for podcasting

- Wireless microphone

- Rode microphone.

Headlines: For keyword-based ads, the headlines must have the actual keyword in the headline. When I say must, I mean it's best practice because it will increase your ad ranking.

Here are some examples of headlines:

- [Your brand name].

- The best podcasting microphone.

- Comes in red or white.

- #1 wireless mic in Australia.

Description: This is the same as your branded Google ad. This should include extra information about your brand and USPs.

Sitelink extensions: This is also the same as the branded Google ad. Link your best-selling products, company information and warranties.

> **Tip**
>
> You can have multiple keyword-based campaigns. For each different product or collection, you can create a new keyword campaign. This will help you see which ones are working well and will keep your account tidy.

Performance max (PMAX) ads

You know when you are about to watch a video on YouTube, but it serves you an ad first? Or when you are browsing a news/blog site and you see ads at the top or between paragraphs? Those are all, most likely, a result of a performance max (PMAX) campaign.

PMAX is an AI-driven, automated Google Ad campaign where, as a business owner, you upload your images and videos, and Google will automatically place them in ad locations across the web. It serves your ad across:

- search ads

- shopping ads

- display ads

- YouTube ads

- Google Maps ads

- Gmail ads.

To create a PMAX campaign, you need to upload your assets, such as images, videos, logos and copy, into the campaign and Google's machine learning will serve and test multiple combinations of those assets to different audiences. It will continue to optimise the combinations until it finds the best one for the right audience.

The best part of PMAX is that it will connect to your website's product catalogue, which means that shopping ads will automatically connect what people are searching for with the products you sell.

Let me talk you through an example:

At Hero Packaging, we have a PMAX campaign that includes all of our products. For this campaign, we have uploaded:

- our logo

- our best lifestyle and product images

- a video explaining our business

- headline variations (e.g., Australia's favourite sustainable packaging)

- descriptions (e.g., Same-day dispatch Australia-wide).

Hero Packaging's PMAX campaigns dynamically show our ads to people across multiple Google platforms. They use AI to optimise different variations of our images, videos and copy, with the goal of getting those people to convert to a sale.

It's a pretty clever campaign!

Tip

Try and give Google as much data as possible, because the more data it has, the faster it can give you the results you want. Focus on uploading the maximum number of videos, images, headlines and descriptions so Google can optimise your ad faster and for the highest return.

CHAPTER 16

MOFU strategy #4: SEO

I want you to search for 'best mountain bike' on Google. Yes, right now. Go and search that and look at the search results. I want you to ignore the shopping ads and the sponsored search ads and, instead, look at the top five organic (non-ad) search results.

These websites displaying 'organically' have worked very hard to be there. They have used search engine optimisation (SEO) strategies to surpass the millions of other articles and posts online and sit on the first page of Google search results for this keyword.

This is because SEO is a long-term, free marketing strategy that can lead hundreds if not thousands of visitors from your target market to your website.

SEO is a set of actions you can do as a business to improve your website's organic (non-paid) visibility in search engines, like Google or Bing, with the goal of getting more organic traffic to your website. But as you know, Google prioritises ads and constantly changes the way search results are displayed, so is SEO for your business even worth it anymore?

Let me give you some stats to answer this question:

- Organic search results get 73 per cent of clicks, while paid ads only get 27 per cent of clicks (BrightEdge, 2023).

- Less than 1 per cent of people go to the second page of Google search results (Backlinko, 2023).

- The first organic search result, on average, gets 39.8 per cent of clicks, while the second and third search results get 18.7 per cent and 10.2 per cent, respectively (Backlinko, 2023).

- The top traffic source, on average, for all websites is organic search (Hubspot, 2023).

So, that answer is 'yes'. It is not only worth it, but it is a strategy that should be prioritised for all businesses.

Now, let's go back to those mountain bike search results. I want you to look at the top three organic search results and take note of:

- Which business owns those websites?

- Are the top results an article, blog post or product page?

- What is the heading of the page?

- How do they use the search term 'best mountain bike' and how often?

This is the start of understanding SEO strategy. Searching for different words and questions that people type into Google, and looking at the top three search results will give you a deeper understanding of what is required to be successful with SEO.

But, how does SEO actually work?

Google uses a set of algorithms to assess and rank different website pages. These algorithms have hundreds of factors within them to determine what the rankings should be. In fact, no one (other than Google) knows exactly what all the factors are. Over the years, Google has officially confirmed the importance of several factors:

- relevant and useful content

- site user experience (UX)

- on-page SEO

- backlinks.

Relevant and useful content

This is, by far, the most important SEO tactic.

Relevant content is about satisfying the user's search intent. In simple terms, your content should answer the question that the person is asking. When it comes to creating relevant content, there are four categories you should always consider:

- navigational (e.g., Hero Packaging mailers)

- informational (e.g., What is compostable packaging?)

- commercial (e.g., Hero Packaging review)

- transactional (e.g., Hero Packaging discount code).

The content on your website needs to make sure that it fulfils the intent of the person searching. For example, if someone types in 'Best men's deodorant in Australia', they don't want to read about an article called 'What is men's deodorant?' While it is talking about the same topic, it is not fulfilling the search intent.

SO, HOW DO YOU KNOW WHAT PEOPLE ARE SEARCHING FOR?

Use a tool like SEMRUSH (paid), Google Keyword Planner (free) or Answer the Public (free). Type in your type of product, for example, 'men's deodorant'.

SEMRUSH will tell you everything you need to know about that keyword:

◆ how many searches per month in any country

◆ all the frequently asked questions about that keyword

◆ the categorisation of that keyword: navigational, informational, commercial or transactional

◆ which websites are ranked in the top ten positions for that keyword.

Google Keyword Planner will show you two main things:

◆ how many people are searching for the keyword in any country

◆ related keywords and keyword phrases.

Answer the Public will give you dozens of questions and statements that people are currently searching in relation to that keyword.

TIME TO WRITE THE SEO COPY

I am about to tell you an SEO secret that not many businesses know about. When you want to write about a particular topic or product, you need to do four separate pieces of writing, not just one. Each one will cover off a search intent category (navigational, informational, commercial, transactional). The pieces of writing could include a blog post, a product page description or a landing page.

This way, you are making sure that whatever search intent someone has about your category or product, you have information that is useful to them.

Let's first go through my exact process on how to write a blog post. Here is what I do:

- Focus on a product or collection.

- Look for the relevant keywords and keyword phrases using Google Keyword Planner.

- Use a tool like Answer the Public to write down five to ten questions that people are searching for in that category.

- Categorise those questions by search intent (navigational, informational, commercial or transactional).

- Choose one intent and focus on answering those specific questions for this blog post.

- Type those questions into Google and take note of the top three organic search results. Are they comparison sites? Are they media articles? Are they product pages? Are they reports? This will guide your content style.

Now use the CURE method to write great SEO content.

THE CURE METHOD

This is a framework I use to help me write blog posts. The CURE method will help your blog post be highly optimised for SEO because it will cover off the four main elements that Google looks for when crawling for valuable and relevant content.

- *Comprehensiveness:* Cover the topic thoroughly and answer all the questions a visitor might have. It's not about word count. Ensure that each page gives searchers a complete resource.

- *Uniqueness:* Your content should not be a compilation of the top results. It should always provide some added value: whether it is a unique angle, useful data, helpful examples or original visuals.

- *Readability:* Your text should be easy to read. This includes structuring your content logically, writing short sentences and having subheadings.

- *Expertise:* Google pays a lot of attention to expertise and authoritativeness. You should provide accurate and reliable information. Be an expert on what you write about.

For product pages, I use the same process, but instead of writing long-form content, I optimise my product descriptions to make sure I am answering the questions that people are searching for with a specific product.

For example, if someone is searching for 'What are compostable mailers?', not only will I write a blog post about that, but in my product description, I will also have a subheading called 'What are compostable mailers' and answer it in short form with useful information.

Site user experience (UX)

Have you ever searched for something on Google, scrolled through the search results, found one that looks like an interesting article only to get to a page that loads slowly, has too much information and has a difficult menu to navigate? It's a terrible experience and it probably leads you to bounce off the site back to the search results to find a different site.

When someone has a bad user experience (UX) and leaves a site to find something better it's called 'pogo sticking', and it's something that negatively affects your search rankings. When people leave a website quickly and go back to Google, it tells Google that the site is not relevant for what was searched. It's a death sentence for search rankings.

So, having relevant content is not enough. Your site needs to provide a great UX too. How do you do that? There are three key things you need to focus on:

PAGE SPEED

Google ranks faster pages higher in the search results because they provide a better UX. A great way to speed up your site is by hiring a freelancer. There are many great sites that have highly skilled and affordable freelancers. It should take them a day to speed it up and cost you about $100 to $300, depending on the complexity of your site. Make sure to check their reviews and previous work before hiring them.

MOBILE FRIENDLINESS

When you are improving your website, always look at your mobile version first. Most website traffic to your website is through mobiles, so your mobile experience should be easy and frictionless. Look at things like your mobile menu, your product pages and your cart to see how they display.

EASE OF USE

Can visitors get to where they want to go quickly? Is it easy to find a product, add to cart, go to checkout and transact? Is it easy to find

MOFU

extra information about other products? Making your site easy to use and navigate makes for a much better experience and tells Google your site is valuable.

The best place to start is to run a site audit. I highly recommend using a tool like SEMRUSH (paid), AHREFS (paid) or Ubersuggest (free) to conduct a website SEO audit. It will look at each of the points above and give you detailed suggestions on how to fix your site to improve usability.

Once you have a list of things you want to fix, you need to spend one to two days focusing on ticking those items off the list. This will immediately help your SEO.

On-page SEO

Imagine you have a very messy house. There are clothes all over the beds and shoes everywhere. You can't find anything that you're looking for. Now imagine that you spend a whole week cleaning up the house and putting the clothes in the right cupboards. All the toys are put away and the shoes get put into shoeboxes and stored neatly. Imagine also that you label everything so that your family can find anything they are looking for.

This is similar to what on-page SEO does for your website. It's like giving your website a makeover to ensure it's easy to find products, quick to load and simple to navigate for both your visitors and search engines. In the digital world, this means making your website fast, ensuring it can be easily explored by search engines, and organising its content in a way that is easy to find and understand. It is the BTS magic that helps your website make a great first impression with any new visitors.

So, what do you need to do to improve your on-page SEO? Let's go through some key pages on your website.

PRODUCT DESCRIPTIONS

Focus on keyword phrases that people would be searching for on Google. For example, if you sell face cream, then your keyword phrase may be 'hydrating cream for ageing skin'. It's important to use this phrase in the first sentence of the description and mention it two to three more times, depending on how long the description is.

The product description is less about word count and more about giving all the right information to the user. Two or three paragraphs is more than enough.

Use frequently asked questions in your description (as subheadings). If people have asked common questions about this product, they are most likely searching for those answers on Google.

TITLE TAGS

A title tag is the main heading for the page that displays in search results. Title tags should ideally have the product name and a keyword (this helps Google understand more about the page); for example, 'hydrating face cream – ageing skin'. Make sure the title tag is less than 60 characters or it may get cut-off in search results.

META DESCRIPTIONS

First, a quick lesson on what meta descriptions are meant to accomplish.

Meta descriptions describe the page to search engines. So, when Google crawls a website, it can easily identify what the page is about. They're also the text that users see when they scan through the search results. The meta description text appears right under the title tag.

You can edit your meta description on your product pages. Here are some tips to improve them:

◆ Add keywords to meta descriptions and focus on making them descriptive and unique to the product. Treat it like an ad and include information about product features, benefits and what problem it solves. Because meta descriptions display in search results, you're trying to entice the user with a good description so they click through to your website.

◆ Every meta description should be different, even if you are writing about very similar products.

◆ Make sure your meta description is under 160 characters long.

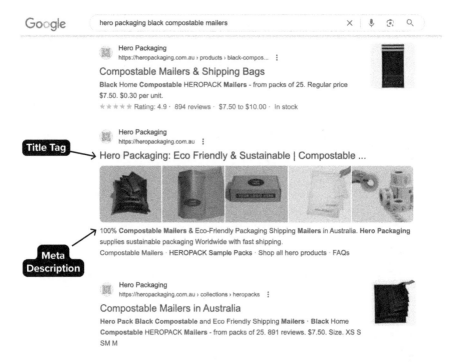

IMAGES

The images on your website contain critical data that is used by Google in its algorithms. There are four elements of product images that you need to improve.

1. IMAGE FILE NAMES

When naming image files, use words that describe the image accurately and clearly. Rather than 'Image01', use 'red-running-shoes'. The name of the image file will help search engines determine what the picture contains. You should include a keyword that you are trying to rank for when writing the image file name; however, avoid making long file names and 'keyword stuffing' (using too many keywords) because this could have a negative effect on ranking. Use dashes to separate words rather than underscores, which will combine words rather than separating them.

2. ALT TEXT

Alt text describes the image to search engines so they can understand them. This is different from the image file name. The image file name is what you have saved the image as, and the alt text usually needs to be added manually on your website. When you are editing a product page, click on an image and you will be able to edit its alt text.

Similar to the image file name, include the product name, some descriptive words, and only use words relevant to the content of the image.

3. IMAGE FILE SIZES

Slow page load times can negatively affect your ranking from search engine algorithms, and image file sizes play a very important role in increasing speed.

Use image sizes at the recommended size for your website platform: for Shopify, the ideal size is 2048px × 2048px. Don't place a large image file on your website and use the HTML code to make it smaller — this will increase load times. Keep file sizes under 70KB.

MOFU

4. IMAGE FILE TYPES

Using the right file types can help keep file sizes lower. JPEG is the most frequently used file type for e-commerce stores because it allows a higher-quality image with a smaller file size.

LINKS

Here is the secret sauce of your product pages. Internally linking product pages to other pages on your site spreads the good SEO juice from page to page and improves the overall SEO of your site.

Say, for example, you have a product page for black tights; however, if you have these same tights in multiple colours (on different product pages), you can link to the various colours in the product description. Maybe you have a blog post that explains the product better. Link to it in the description!

COLLECTIONS/CATEGORY PAGE DESCRIPTIONS

I have seen thousands of collections pages over the years, and more than 75 per cent of them don't have a description. But, did you know that collections pages are actually more important than product pages for SEO? Not having a description on these pages lowers the chance of Google indexing the page to show up in the search results.

Collection page descriptions work in the same way as product descriptions. They should focus on what the collection is, what products it has and keywords that users are typing into Google. They should also include links to products within the collection. This is to spread that SEO juice to more pages on your site.

Two to three paragraphs are all you need, and you can choose to put the description at the bottom of the page so it doesn't affect the user experience.

BLOG POSTS

All of us know we should be writing blog posts frequently. We know they are good for SEO, but let's be honest, they can be a real pain in the neck and most of us tend to put them on the back burner. This is not just because they take time to research and write, but the results from writing them aren't seen for weeks or months.

But blog posts are critical when it comes to SEO. They can contain detailed answers that visitors are looking for that aren't on your product pages. They can also show your expertise and authority in an industry.

My suggestion is to aim for two blog posts per week. Build it into your marketing plan every week because they can significantly influence the number of people who visit your website. Here are the main elements you need to include in your blog posts:

- *A great title:* It needs to describe exactly what the blog post is about. Let's say your blog post is about ab exercises you can do at home. Rather than using a TikTok-style hook like, 'You won't believe what gave me a six pack', create a clear title like 'Three effective ab exercises you can do at home'.

- *Keyword inclusion:* Ideally, place the keyword that you are focusing on as close to the start of the blog post. Google is known to put more value on words at the top of the page.

- *Image file names and alt tags:* Make sure that at least one of the images contains the targeted keyword in the file name.

- *Word count:* A blog post should have more than 1000 words. According to CoSchedule (2024), the ideal length is 2500 words.

- *Links in blog posts:* You should be including links in your blog posts. If you have sourced information from another website, it is important to link to them to credit their work. But, most importantly, I would like you to link internally to other pages on your website. If your blog post is talking about something you sell, make sure you link to it. These internal links can really help with your SEO.

Backlinks

Have you ever seen a recipe online where each ingredient is a link to a website where you can buy it? Those links are known as backlinks, and they are first and foremost very useful to the reader of the article because it helps them find the right information online. But these links also help businesses because any website containing a link back to your website is like a vote of confidence in your website. These links could be from blog posts or news articles. They tell Google that another website likes you and vouches for you.

In very general terms, the more backlinks you have from other websites, the better your SEO results. Unfortunately, not all backlinks are created equal. A news site, for example, has much more credibility than a small business listing website, so having a backlink from that news site is much better for your SEO.

There are many ways to get backlinks, but in all honesty, most of them are time-consuming, tedious and are definitely not sustainable for you as a business owner. Let's go through four genuine backlink strategies that you can actually do:

HOW CAN PR HELP SEO?

Getting PR for your business serves two key purposes: it gets you brand awareness and it improves your SEO. The latter is rarely spoken about because it's not exciting, but getting featured in blogs, news articles and other online publications can drastically improve your search rankings.

SHAREABLE STATS

This is a trick I learnt at an SEO conference. One of the speakers said that by gathering cool stats and data, and publishing it on your website, you can attract a lot of shares.

For example, say you sell skincare and you survey your email database about a topic like dry skin. You may find out that 70 per cent of people surveyed have dry skin and are confused about skincare for dry skin.

That's a fantastic, unique, shareable stat that beauty editors and bloggers would love to know and use in their online content.

Publish a blog post on your site with that stat as the central point. Talk about it on social media and direct people to your post. Over time, it will start to get noticed and shared by other online sites. More backlinks acquired!

COLLAB WITH OTHER BRANDS

This is an easy one and kind of fun too! It's a simple backlink exchange. Find a brand that is similar to yours or one that you've partnered with before. Ask them to write a blog post on you and link back to your site, and you do the same for them.

Do that with five brands every month and you get 60 great backlinks a year!

HIRE SOMEONE

Of course, I have to put this strategy in here. It's the easiest one of all, but it does require payment.

Most large companies pay an SEO company to improve their search rankings. What they don't really know is that they are mainly paying for backlink generation.

Rather than paying an agency over $2000 per month, head over to a freelancer website and find an SEO expert. For a fraction of the cost, that expert can start acquiring backlinks for you through guest posting. It's fast and effective.

Remember when I said that not all backlinks are created equal? Well, this is the time to make sure you are getting the right backlinks. When you hire a freelancer, make sure you tell them that you only want 'white hat' backlinks. These are backlinks with a good 'domain authority' score on Google. Ideally, you want backlinks from websites with domain authorities greater than 25.

CHAPTER 17

MOFU strategy #5: Instagram

In late 2023, I wanted to host a marketing masterclass. It was a free virtual event where my audience would learn about social media tips for an hour. I did two things to drive sign-ups:

1. I sent an email to 5000 subscribers.

2. I created an Instagram story with a link on the screen (it received 4000 story views).

Which one do you think had the most clicks and signups?

Surprisingly, it was my Instagram stories. I have been working on my Instagram story strategy for a long time, and I have figured out what receives the most views and the most engagement. When I want to drive people to my website, Instagram stories is a major driver.

What I love about Instagram is that it has multiple functions. It can be used to build brand awareness, create an educational platform, foster a community and, most importantly for this chapter, drive people to your website.

But most brand owners don't know how to leverage the right parts of Instagram for each goal. A mistake I see is that when a business owner wants their audience to visit a product page or sign up for a launch or giveaway, they ask their audience to do it from a post or a reel.

How many times have you seen the words 'click the link in our bio to sign up' or 'click the link in our bio to see our new collection' in a caption? This is asking for a person to click their business name (click number 1), then click the link in the bio (click number 2), then click the button on their Linktree (click number 3) before they finally get to the website. That is way too many clicks and way too much of an interruption to their scroll. You lost them at the first click!

Directing your audience to your website through posts and reels is not the best way. Reels and posts should be used to get more brand visibility with a new audience or to nurture your current audience. If you want your audience to click through to your website, you need to use Instagram stories.

My best Instagram stories tips

Instagram stories is where you really build connection with your audience. To make them effective, each story needs to have one clear message — keeping them simple makes it easy for the audience to consume your content and take action. When you want viewers to click the button (to get them to your website), here are my top tips:

◆ Make sure that you have the specific link you want to use. Don't simply link to your homepage or a generic collections page. If you are going to direct people to your site, direct them to exactly where they need to go.

◆ Add the link sticker on the first story you do. If you want the maximum number of people clicking on the link, don't hide it in your sixth or seventh story. There is usually a 10 to 20 per cent drop-off rate between stories, and you won't see a high click-through rate after your first story.

◆ Use only one link, sticker or button per story. Instagram gives you the option to tag people, use hashtags, have a question box, add a link and add a product button in your stories. If you use two or more in one story, the clicks will be divided between them, and you won't get 100 per cent of your audience going to the place you actually want them to go to.

◆ Understand how your audience responds to your stories. Do you get more story views when you use a photo, a video or text on screen? On my accounts, the difference in views is in the thousands. Knowing this will help you understand what type of story to post to get the most views and, therefore, the most clicks.

OK, so you have loads of people flowing through your TOFU, you have potential customers warming up in your MOFU, and now comes the final and most important part of the process. Progressing those 'warm' potential customers from the MOFU into the BOFU and converting them into paying customers!

MOFU

Q&A with James Reu, former head of e-commerce, LSKD

A self-described e-commerce fanatic, James has seen it all—from small agencies to global head offices. In his previous role as the head of e-commerce, he took LSKD's online experience and retention strategy to a new level, implementing personalisation, loyalty, reviews, on-site search and a mobile app that claimed the top position on the iOS App Store's shopping chart. James's efforts have resulted in significant growth for the business. I asked him about product strategy, marketing and the future of e-commerce.

If you could attribute LSKD's rapid growth in the last couple of years to a few strategies, what would they be?

One of LSKD's growth strategies is to consistently introduce something new and engaging to our community. Whether it's new products, a promotion or events, these strategies keep the community engaged with the brand. Additionally, we place a strong emphasis on support and fostering meaningful relationships with our customers, which makes them feel a part of who we are as a brand.

There is so much competition in the activewear space. Why do you think LSKD has stood out?

LSKD distinguishes itself through emotionally engaging storytelling. We focus on selling a feeling or experience rather than just a product. Our brand is built around the mission to be '1 per cent better every day', which resonates deeply with our audience. Our mission helps us connect on a more personal level and to set the standard in the activewear space.

There must be so many people at any given time sitting in your MOFU—what strategies do you use to convert those people from just knowing about you to actually purchasing from you?

Our mid-funnel conversion strategy is multi-faceted, focusing on deepening the connection between brand and consumer; how we can help them, not just sell to them. For example, we leverage targeted content to further educate consumers on the unique benefits of our products; UGC [user-generated content] and social proof is also a massive driver of this. A first-purchase discount is then offered as a direct response strategy, encouraging them to take action.

I've never quite seen a product or sale launch like LSKD's before. How many months of planning does it take to execute launches?

From content creation to email marketing to Facebook ads, everything is so in sync. How is this all mapped out? Do you use a project management tool?

We often refer to the term 'win before launch', meaning we have planted the seed for success. Product drops are organised months in advance and plotted out using our planning software. Our marketing team uses this planning to create a compelling story and strategy around the drop. For larger promotions, like Black Friday, collaboration across all departments is essential to ensure a seamless event. We generate initial interest through 'coming soon' messaging and interest registration, allowing us to refine our projections. Additionally, we prepare our technology infrastructure to handle increased traffic, ensuring stability and responsiveness during high-traffic periods.

What piece of marketing advice would you give a business owner wanting to scale their e-commerce store?

Building a network is crucial. It's beneficial to learn from those who've been in your shoes. Platforms like LinkedIn, Facebook Groups, X and others are great for connecting with the e-commerce leaders and founders.

Collaboration is key in today's e-commerce world. Partnering with other brands can open up new audiences and tell a unique story to your customers, offering a fresh level of exposure and expanding your customer base.

I wouldn't shy away from selling out of a collection strategically. Creating a sense of scarcity can attract highly engaged customers who don't want to miss out on what you're selling. People place more value on products that are harder to get.

What are your predictions for the future of e-commerce?

Brand websites may become less dominant in the future due to the increasing popularity of social commerce platforms, like Instagram and TikTok, where users can discover and purchase products seamlessly within their social feeds. Additionally, the continued expansion and dominance of retail giants like Amazon could further marginalise standalone e-commerce websites by offering more convenience, variety and competitive pricing.

STAGE 3

Converting customers in the BOFU

The easiest way for you to make money in your business is to convert those people who already want to buy, but never have.

In 2023, after months of negotiation with one of our manufacturers, we were able to reduce the cost of one of our best-selling products, our padded mailers, by 15 per cent. At Hero Packaging, we have always believed in sharing wins with our customers, so we decided to pass on a portion of that cost saving to our customers and potential customers. We permanently reduced the price of that product, and we emailed our database to let them know.

Within six hours, we had 127 orders for padded mailers. Out of these, 92 orders were placed by people who had never bought from us before. Those 92 people had been waiting on the sidelines, ready to buy. They

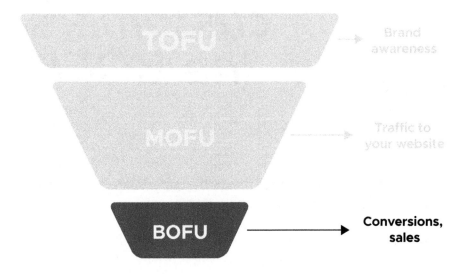

were looking for one little incentive to push them over the edge, and our small price reduction got them there.

But converting this 'hot' audience is not just about price reduction and discounts. It is about a multitude of strategies that can be implemented to turn them from a visitor into a customer.

Strategies in this part of the funnel focus on persuasion, both subtle and direct. The first and most important part of this section is your website optimisation. You want the UX to be easy and wonderful. This, in turn, creates a high-converting website, so that when you drive traffic using your TOFU and MOFU strategies, your website is working the hardest it possibly can to convert visitors into customers.

BOFU

CHAPTER 18

BOFU strategy #1: Website optimisation

In one of my mentoring calls, I had a client say to me: 'I have hundreds of people coming to my website every day, but I only get two to three sales. Am I doing something wrong?'

I had a look through their website, and immediately noticed some things that needed to be fixed. The site speed was slow, and her mobile menu wasn't working smoothly. Her product images were sized differently, and she had no videos on her site. Overall, it gave the impression that her business wasn't very professional or trustworthy. I made a list of changes that she needed to make, and over the period of a week she worked through them. In one week, her conversation rate went from 1 per cent to 2.6 per cent. As she continued to add more photos to her product pages and more detailed copy, her conversion rate grew to 3.2 per cent. This meant that she went from two to three daily sales to over nine. She tripled her revenue with no extra spend.

This process of fixing your website is called website optimisation or conversion rate optimisation (CRO), and it is measured using your conversion rate. You can calculate conversion rate by dividing the number of daily orders by the number of daily website visitors and multiplying by 100.

$$\frac{\text{Number of daily orders}}{\text{Number of daily website visitors}} \times 100 = \text{conversion rate}$$

For example, if a business has about 200 visitors to its website in one day and receives four orders, then its conversion rate for that day is 2 per cent.

$$\frac{4}{200} \times 100 = 2$$

In late 2023, Shopify announced that the average conversion rate on their stores was 1.4 per cent. That means for every 100 people that visit a store, there are between one and two orders. It doesn't sound like a lot, but you have to remember that people can come to your website for many reasons and not just to place an order. They may come to browse, to enquire, to learn more, to enter a giveaway, to check order information, to speak to someone on live chat or to place an order.

However, I like to see conversion rates of at least 2.5 to 3 per cent. This is a good starting point for brands to see a good number of conversions every day.

To increase conversion rates, there are hundreds of things you can do, but I have compiled a list of my top ways to convert more website visitors into customers.

Before you make any changes

There are three things I need you to do before you make any changes to your website.

Before you start changing anything on your website, you need to use a heatmap. A heatmap is an incredible tool that shows you what your website visitors are clicking on and interacting with on your website. It gives you a colour-coded representation of the interactions: things that are clicked on the most turn red and elements that are least interacted with turn blue. When you see what people are actually clicking on (and not), you get a clear picture of what you need to update and change on your site. To use a heatmap, download a tool such as Microsoft Clarity or Hotjar and connect your website.

The second thing you need to do is think mobile first. I often see business owners make changes on the desktop version of their site, but as approximately 90 per cent of shoppers are on their mobiles, it makes sense to start with the mobile site. The tips I'm about to share with you work across both the mobile and desktop sites.

Third, you must fix your site speed. This is the foundation of having a high-converting website. You can either try and do it yourself by resizing images and removing plugins, or you can use a website developer or freelancer to help you. It will usually cost around $50 to $100 and take less than a day. Make sure to use someone who has lots of great reviews, and ensure they always download a backup of your website before making changes.

Let's get into the nitty gritty conversion rate tips!

BOFU

Homepage

Your homepage is where most of your website visitors land, so this is the place I want you to start in your CRO journey! Making small changes to your homepage can result in big changes to your order volume. The main job of your homepage is to keep people on your website, as well as direct them to what they need quickly. Imagine walking into a department store and not having proper signage for each section, or not having enough space to easily walk through the store. Your website is no different: you need to make sure people can find what they need in two clicks or less.

Here are my top tips to optimise your homepage:

The top announcement bar: Essential info

The top announcement bar sits above your header, and features essential information, such as shipping information; contact details; or an announcement of something exciting, like a storewide discount. It's one of the first things your visitors see and it's also visible on every page, so use this space wisely!

Here are some examples you can use:

- All orders are shipped within 24 hours

- We have same-day shipping before 2pm, everyday

- Flash sale 40 per cent off sitewide!

- Free shipping AND free returns.

The header: The face of your brand

The header is the face of your brand. Ensure your logo is high resolution. This area should include an easy-to-click menu, a search bar for quick product searches, and a cart icon.

The menu: Your store's roadmap

Keep it simple. Always start by looking at the mobile menu first. Each collection and product should be one click away, and consider naming your collections exactly what they are and not anything abstract. For example, let's say you sell jewellery and you create a collection with star signs on necklaces, instead of opting for an abstract name like 'Karma Collection', name it something like 'Astrology Necklaces Collection' or 'Star Sign Necklaces'. This will make the website much easier to navigate for your customers. For your desktop menu, consider using a smart menu, which has images as well as text and helps visitors to navigate your site easily.

The value bar: Showcase your unique selling proposition (USP)

Situated right under the header, this bar is your chance to highlight your USP. Warranty information, return and exchange policies, buy-now pay-later options, certifications — these are the assurances that answer common customer objections. The value bar on the Hero Packaging website includes three USPs: 20 per cent of profits donated, same-day dispatch, Afterpay and ZipPay.

Main banner: First impressions count

This is the first image you see on a website, and it is the first impression someone has of your website. Choose a high-impact, high-resolution image or video of one product or one collection. One of the things I always advise business owners is to not use a Canva-designed image for your main banner. It is usually not high quality and can make a bad first impression. Instead, showcase a lifestyle image and use the text field to write the copy and the CTA. Make sure the CTA is clear; for example, 'Shop our best-selling cap'. The CTA is best displayed as a button. Showpo always has excellent main banners, so go to their website to get inspiration.

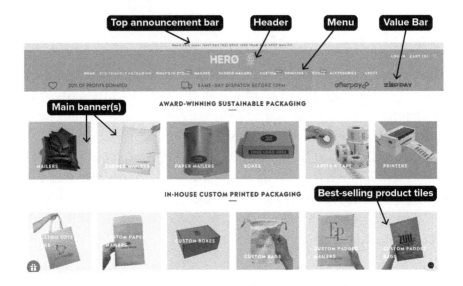

Product tiles or collection tiles:
Your bestsellers on display

Feature six to eight product or collection tiles showcasing your bestsellers or new releases. Enable customers to add products to their cart right from these tiles, eliminating the need for extra clicks.

SHOPPABLE VIDEOS: MAKE YOUR WEBSITE ITS OWN SOCIAL MEDIA PLATFORM

Use tools like GoTolstoy to integrate shoppable videos on your homepage. They're not just engaging; they boost SEO and offer innovative ways for product discovery and customer interaction, such as quizzes.

TWO-CLICK NAVIGATION: LESS IS MORE

The key here is accessibility. Make sure your customers can get to the product they want within two clicks. Imagine if a customer has seen a social media post where you are showcasing a red dress. That customer clicks through to your homepage and looks for that red dress. They try clicking on 'new arrivals', but can't find it. They try clicking on 'dresses', but there are too many and they still can't find it. That customer is going to get frustrated and leave your site. You must make it easy for them to get to where they need to go by utilising filters on collections pages, optimising the search functionality and including bestsellers in the menu.

THE FOOTER: FORGOTTEN REAL ESTATE

Don't forget the footer! When you look through your heatmap, you'll notice that at least 10 per cent of visitors click on a link in the footer, but it's an area of the website that's often forgotten. Include FAQs, shipping details, links to social media, and an About Us section. If you have certifications in your business, it's a great place to showcase them using icons.

Product pages

The goal of your product page is to get people to add products to cart. It requires persuasion in the form of subtle cues (like image quality and reviews), visual impact and convincing copy. Here are my tips to ensure your product pages are converting highly.

Consistency in image shapes

Your product images must all be the same shape and size (all squares or all rectangles). Maintaining a uniform shape is a subtle cue to visitors that your site is professional. On Shopify, the ideal image size is 2048px × 2048px, but you can also upload up to 4472px × 4472px as long as the file size is under 20MB. When choosing a consistent image size, you also need to balance the file size of each image, as this affects your website speed and can reduce conversion. Try finding a sweet spot where your images are 2048px × 2048px with a file size of around 100KB to 150KB each.

BOFU

A range of image types

It is not good enough to have only one image for your products. Each product should ideally have six to eight images and videos to really showcase the product in use. Here are the image types I highly recommend:

- E-commerce images: These are straightforward product shots, typically against a plain-coloured background, such as white, black or grey. E-commerce shots are usually the first images for a product page to make it look more professional. Another reason to use e-commerce images is because Google Shopping doesn't allow other types of images, such as lifestyle images or images where there is too much text, to appear in the Google Shopping feed.

- Lifestyle images: These images show the product in use, often in real-life scenarios.

- Detail images: These are close-up shots that highlight the quality and features of the product. Think about brands like Rolex that use detailed images to showcase the craftsmanship of their watches.

- User-generated content: This includes real-life images or videos from customers. A company that does this really well is GoPro. They feature adventurous videos and images taken by their customers. There is nothing more convincing than seeing other customers enjoying your product.

- Before-and-after images: This is not just for fashion or skincare! I know we are used to seeing brands like L'Oreal using before-and-after photos, but every brand can use them, and they are powerful! If you are an artist, you can show a wall with a painting that doesn't suit the room and then show the same room with your artwork. Think outside the box.

Descriptive product names

The product title should include the name, but also a distinctive feature. Dyson, for example, names its products with specific features, such as 'Dyson V11 Torque Drive Cordless Vacuum Cleaner', which is informative, easily searchable and is also excellent for SEO.

Buy-now, pay-later options

Displaying flexible payment options like Klarna, Afterpay or ZipPay near the 'add to cart' button can increase conversions. Luckily, many of these software companies automatically place their logos on your product pages when you sign up. You need to make sure they are prominent and visible above the fold (the part of the screen visible before you scroll).

Reviews and social proof

This is perhaps one of the most important sections on your product page. Use a review app to automatically collect reviews after customers make a purchase. Make sure the star rating is visible near the 'add to cart' button and the full reviews are shown further down the page. A tip is to pull out some wonderful customer quotes and use them as features on the product page.

Size chart

This is not just for fashion brands. A size chart is commonly used for apparel, such as T-shirts, shorts, dresses etc., but it can actually be used for most products. For example, a brand selling lipsticks might include a colour chart. Or for packaging, it might explain what fits inside each box. I see many size charts that just have a table with measurements. I want you to put yourself in your customer's shoes and think about what they really need. They want to know whether that dress is going to fit them properly. The size chart is a great way to

BOFU

show more detail. You can have models of different sizes showcasing the dress, and you can talk about the stretch of the fabric or the fit (is it loose or tight). Create a comprehensive size chart for each product.

High-contrast add-to-cart button

The 'add to cart' button should be in a high-contrast colour to the rest of your site. Amazon uses a bright orange for its button, which stands out against its white background. Many tests have been done between low-contrast and high-contrast buttons, and conversion rates are much higher with a bolder button.

Subscription sales

Turning single-purchase items into subscription offerings can ensure recurring revenue and customer retention. It is now really easy to add a subscription service to your website if you use an app like Yotpo. For example, Dollar Shave Club revolutionised the razor market by offering convenient, regular deliveries through subscription models.

Accordion-style product description

A collapsible menu helps organise large amounts of information without overwhelming the user. Within your product description, you want to have as much information as possible about your product, but having a lot of text isn't exactly aesthetically pleasing. An accordion menu can include extra text like FAQs, warranty information, and shipping and returns into sections that can be expanded. It's cleaner and easier to digest.

Product-specific FAQs

Every product should have a list of specific FAQs related to it. Take note of what customers ask about certain products when they email you and document them in an FAQ section on each product page. These FAQs can pre-emptively address customer queries and concerns, and remove obstacles to purchase. It also helps to minimise customer emails.

TACKLE OBJECTIONS

I want you to pick three reasons why visitors would *not* buy your product. Some examples could be that they are worried about the returns policy, they don't think they will receive it quickly or they are unsure about the quality. Use these as a focus on your product page by directly answering them with bold text and icons. Addressing these common customer objections can significantly increase conversion rates and lower customer service enquiries. Patagonia, for example, quickly handles potential objections by highlighting their ethical practices and lifetime warranty, reassuring customers about the quality and sustainability of their purchases.

Frequently bought together

Suggesting complementary products based on what others have bought together can increase the average order value. New visitors don't know anything about the other products that you sell, so it's a great opportunity to tell them what products work well with the one they are currently looking at. Amazon is known for its 'frequently bought together' section, which cleverly suggests additional items that complement the primary product, encouraging additional purchases. It's done through AI, which uses data to suggest products. There are many apps on the Shopify App Store that perform very similar functions.

Shoppable videos

These interactive videos on your product page are a great way to talk more about the product or answer customer questions. You can add a video of you talking to camera or use user-generated videos.

BOFU

Activewear brands, such as LSKD, use these to create an engaging shopping experience, allowing customers to see the clothes in action.

Comparison charts

Provide a visual comparison between your product compared with competitor products. This is best in a table format where you list various features and benefits with one column representing your brand and another representing competitor brands. In your column, there should be a lot of ticks, and there should be crosses in the competitor column. It's a great visual tool to persuade visitors to shop with you.

Collections pages

Your collections pages include products that fit into a category, such as dresses, shoes, preschool toys, business books and so on. Its main function is to act as a map for customers to easily navigate your website and get to the product they want quickly. There are a few key changes you can make to optimise your collections pages.

Display all collections

If a visitor goes to a collections page, it is beneficial to show all collections at the top of the page so they can click through to each one without having to go back to the main menu.

Filters

This is by far the most important feature on your collections pages. Have a great filtering system where customers can filter as many features as possible, such as size, material, style, scent, event, colour, price, measurements, etc. Most website platforms, such as Shopify, allow you to easily add tags to products to allow for this filtering.

This means you need to add consistent tags to each product in your store.

Include product details

Rather than simply having photos of products, make sure you have key information under each product tile, such as the product name, price and star reviews. This allows a customer to get the information they need without clicking into each product page. You can even go one step further and add filters, such as colour, so people can quickly switch between colours without viewing each individual product page.

Add-to-cart button

Enable an add-to-cart button under each product tile and its key information. If a visitor knows exactly what they want, they can skip the product page altogether and head straight to the cart to purchase.

BOFU

Cart

Your shopping cart has two main functions: to cross-sell or upsell, and to move customers to checkout. Here are some key things your cart should have:

Upsell cart

Use your cart as an opportunity to upsell or cross-sell. You can use an app like Monster Upsells to incentivise the purchase of more products. This is done in three ways:

1. You can have a prize bar at the top of the app, so customers can see that if they spend more, they get more prizes (these could be free shipping or a discount). You may have seen similar promotions along the lines of 'spend $100, save $10'.

2. You can add in bulk ordering in the app: if someone buys two or three products instead of one, they get a discount.

3. The last way is to include a one-click upsell: you can include your cheapest product here and customers can click the circle to add it to their cart.

Display payment options and warranties

Your cart should remind people that they can trust your store, so displaying payment options and warranty information is critical here.

Shipping information

A common reason visitors abandon their cart is because they aren't sure of the shipping time and cost. To prevent this, include text such as: 'Your order will be shipped by…' If you have standard shipping or free shipping, make sure you tell them here too.

Frequently bought together with

New visitors may not have any idea of the other products you sell. It's a great time to introduce them to products that are commonly bought with the one they are about to purchase. Having a 'frequently bought together with' section can increase your average order value (AOV) significantly.

CHAPTER 19

BOFU strategy #2: Email marketing

While the purpose of your website is to convince customers to buy, the reason for your email marketing is to drive consumers to your site, and this is equally as important.

Email marketing at this stage of the funnel is an easy way to persuade consumers to purchase from your store. They have already shown interest by adding products to their cart, now they just need a tiny push to make the transaction.

At this stage, you want to make sure you have automated email flows set up to capture visitors. These will automatically get sent to customers based on their previous behaviour, and will continue to generate sales in the background — no daily work required!

Cart abandonment email flow

Let's say your customer gets as far as adding an item to their shopping cart, but maybe they get called away to check an email or made a cup of coffee, and they never get to the checkout. A cart abandonment flow will send them a reminder email with the exact products they had in their cart. It removes any barriers that keep the potential customer from completing their purchase.

I recommend setting up two emails in this flow: one that is sent soon after they abandon their cart, and another that is sent a few days later.

Abandoned cart email 1

Trigger: Someone abandons their cart.

Time: Two to three hours later.

Messaging: The ideal abandoned cart automation populates the email with dynamic content, which includes an image and title/description of the product they left in their cart. Dynamic content is unique to each website visitor as it is based on the specific products they added to their cart. You should also add extra copy at the top of the email ensuring it channels your brand's personality.

You can use copy such as:

- You left something behind.

- Did you forget me?

- You are so close to receiving your new favourite product!

- Don't forget to get these before they're gone.

Abandoned cart email 2

Trigger: Someone abandons their cart.

Time: Two to three days later (depending on the product you sell).

Messaging: This will be very similar to the first email with the dynamic content, but this one can be more time sensitive. Saying something like 'This product will sell out soon' or 'Your cart is reserved for another 60 minutes' works well with these emails.

In this email, many businesses send a discount code, but I don't recommend doing this. While it will incentivise customers to make the purchase, customers are smart and may abandon their carts in the future so they can get a discount code in a few days.

BOFU

CHAPTER 20

BOFU strategy #3: TikTok Shop

Imagine you are scrolling through TikTok and see one of your favourite creators reviewing a lipstick, giving it a glowing review. You would have traditionally left the TikTok app, Googled the lipstick and brand, clicked on a website only to see that the lipstick is sold out, returned back to Google and tried another website, clicked through to the product page, added to cart and then purchased the lipstick. You go back to TikTok and keep scrolling until you see another product you want to buy, and the process starts again. Each time you leave the app, it's a disruption to the browsing experience. But TikTok Shop changes all of that.

TikTok Shop is one of the most exciting things to happen to e-commerce in recent times. TikTok has made it possible for your audience to shop your products directly from the TikTok app without clicking through to a website.

A business can upload some or all of its products to TikTok. When a business uploads a video about a certain product, it can tag the product, so whoever sees the video can click on the shopping cart icon on the bottom of the screen and quickly purchase it. The key word here is *quickly*. TikTok allows viewers to shop with a few clicks without ever leaving the TikTok app.

How do you set it up?

The process is very straightforward and easy. Start at shop.tiktok.com and click on 'I am a seller'. You will need to fill in your details to get approved. The approval process can take up to 24 hours.

Once you have been approved as a seller, you will be able to login to your TikTok Shop dashboard, and add your products. You can either do this manually or you can link your current website platform (such as Shopify) to your shop. You may need an app, such as AfterShip Feed for Shopify, to help with this.

You will then be able to see all your products. It will ask you to map the products, which is where you select the products that you want in your TikTok shop and choose the category that they fall under (e.g., cosmetics, haircare, furniture). It will ask for more details about each product, including the size and variants. The more information you provide, the better the product listing will be. Now, click 'sync' and TikTok will start syncing your products to the shop. This could take another 24 hours to get approved.

When it has been approved, the last step is to connect your TikTok shop to your TikTok account. It's an easy connection process and the instructions walk you through it step-by-step.

Congratulations, you now have a TikTok shop!

To see it in action, head over to your TikTok app and you'll now be able to see the shop icon above your videos on your profile page. Tagging a product in a TikTok video is incredibly easy. After you create a video, you need to click on 'add link' and then 'product' and then choose the product you want to link. When you publish the video, viewers will be able to see the shop icon and shop that product directly from your video.

I believe TikTok shop will revolutionise the way people shop online because it can take someone seamlessly from a browsing mindset to a purchasing mindset.

> **Tip**
>
> Setting up a TikTok shop (or shop on any other social media platform) is not a 'set and forget' project. This is an extension of your main website and must be maintained to ensure the product information is correct, images are appearing perfectly and there are no errors in your shop. This also applies to when you're selling on marketplaces, such as Amazon—you need to manage your product information and ensure everything is consistent with your main website.

BOFU

Q&A with Daniel Flynn, co-founder of Thankyou

Daniel Flynn is the co-founder and managing director of one of Australia's most successful startups, Thankyou.

He co-founded Thankyou in 2008 at the age of 19; in 2024 Thankyou's products are stocked by most major retailers in Australia, with every product contributing to help end global poverty. To date, Thankyou has raised over $17 million to improve the lives of people across 22 countries.

Daniel is also the author of best-selling book *Chapter One*, a story that generated $1.4 million in sales in its first month using an unorthodox 'pay-what-you-want' model. He is known for his disruptive marketing and has received widespread media coverage for some truly unconventional and highly successful campaigns that led to Thankyou products being stocked by some of Australia's biggest retailers.

Daniel's achievements as an entrepreneur have also been widely celebrated. In 2014, he was named an honoree in the JCI Ten Outstanding Young People of the World program, and in 2015, Daniel won the Southern region Ernst & Young Entrepreneur of the Year. In 2017, Daniel was named in the Forbes Asia 30 Under 30 for Social Entrepreneurship.

I spoke to him about building communities around your brand — with a difference — and standing out in a crowded market.

What are the key strategies you use to build a community around Thankyou?

At Thankyou, we're a community built on the foundation of purpose and this simple idea that, together, we can make a collective big impact if we each bring what's in our hand to the table. And when we talk about what's in your hand, this is anything from your weekly purchase decision in your grocery shop where you choose to add a Thankyou product, to sharing our stories and message online, through to individuals who might be contributing in bigger ways through partnerships or manufacturing, and beyond.

The key strategy to building this has been inviting people, again and again and again, and showing people the difference that they can make by contributing to this idea. Over time, as our track record has been built, it's led to more belief and more confidence in us and our community, and people continue to get around the idea.

At Thankyou, at times from a community perspective, we've lost momentum, and rebuilding this has been about resharing the vision, resharing the track record of the past and the difference we've made together, and showing consumers the future difference we could make if people were to continue to build with us.

What are some of the best things you can do to create exceptional customer experience from pre-purchase to post-purchase?

Over the years, we've found that sometimes the greatest consumer movement comes when we've invited people in on the journey before a product has launched, whilst it's still in the ideation phase. An example of this was in our Coles and Woolworths campaign. We invited consumers to help us pitch the products that we'd made to major retailers through social media before the products were in-market.

The second time, we did this through launching a book called *Chapter One* that crowdfunded money for us to launch a new category (our baby range) into supermarkets and across the country. This is a really interesting concept where our consumers gain a sense of purpose from being brought in on the process, and it further helps because, when a product hits the shelves, people show up to buy it because they helped get it there.

At Thankyou, we have worked hard and continue to work hard at making our post-purchase experience a good one. From the products we make, the messages and the communications that we send to the community we're building.

In a competitive landscape, how do you stand out? What draws customers back to you over and over again?

It is a competitive landscape and it can be so hard to cut through, but even more than that, it's hard to last over time. But the secrets to getting there are ultimately the fundamentals: great product and great brand. When it comes to products, we live by two rules at Thankyou. Rule one: Make great product. Rule two: Never break rule one.*

And rule two has a little asterisk, and it says, '*Never use a good cause to sell an average product'. We got this idea from an incredible book called *Why Brands With a Purpose Do Better and Matter More*. It's been foundational to everything we do

BOFU

because customers want great products, and if you can deliver that, people will come back for it. Some of our best products just grow year on year — it's a really good product and people know it.

But making a great product that is expensive doesn't work; we've experienced that. There's this balance between the quality of the product and delivering it at a price that works for consumers. That's a hard line to walk because in the competitive landscape, people are willing to discount their product to try and get consumers in. That is one of the great challenges we find in the current environment, but we know that if we deliver a great product, which is our brand promise, that will help us be sustainable long-term.

And from a brand perspective, how do we stand out? Well, we think unconventionally. We think about ideas, and we think about paths forward that others have never seen before, in a way to, in part, stand out. But, also to remind people that Thankyou is different — this is not just another hand wash company, this is not just another 'insert consumer brand'. This idea is different and, as we market and communicate as a brand, we want it to feel different as well, because it is.

Reflecting on Thankyou's journey, what advice would you offer to small business owners who want to increase customer loyalty?

Change your mindset from the idea of 'you' the brand, 'you' the small business and 'they' the customers, and you transition to this idea of 'we' — 'we' the brand builder. All of a sudden, customers aren't the people you are selling to, customers are the people who you're building with. It may seem like a subtle difference, but I think it matters because it affects the way you communicate, the way you take people on the journey and the way you may, transparently, share the challenges and the things that didn't work. We aim to do this at Thankyou, and we've built incredible customer loyalty over the years because of this.

PART III

The secret sauce

You now have people flowing through your funnel and turning into customers. Well done! You should be seeing more orders flowing in and more consistent sales.

Now, I am about to get to my favourite part—the secret sauce to any business.

Your secret sauce is your ability to turn customers into loyal and raving fans. I am going to show you how to make your customers feel incredibly special and give them a remarkable brand experience every time they shop with you. In this section, we will also go through how to build a community from scratch and how to create a bond with your best customers.

Our goal is to create brand advocates and use their word of mouth to promote your business in an organic and wonderful way.

Let me show you how it's done!

How to get your customers to buy from you again

Giving your customers exactly what they ordered and nothing more is the business version of a school report card that says 'met expectations'. You have delivered on what was required, nothing more and nothing less.

Unfortunately, in this crowded market, where every business is competing for customer attention, your product alone, no matter how good it is, is not enough to get customers to return to your store. It is the 'experience' they have when buying from you that keeps customers coming back.

When I teach marketing to students at university, I have to teach them the four Ps of marketing: product, price, placement and promotion. For over six decades, these four Ps have been taught as the fundamentals of marketing. However, I always make a small change when I talk about the first P. Product is no longer just the physical product, it also includes the packaging, the thank you note, the little gift inside, the speed of dispatch and delivery, the customer service, the thank you email, and the discount code for the next order. It is the overall experience from pre-purchase to post-purchase.

As business owners, it seems unfair to have to provide that experience when the customer has only paid for the product. But let me tell you this, those customers haven't just paid with their money — they have spent time researching your product, looking at alternatives, comparing brands and, ultimately, choosing yours. They have not just paid with money, but also their time and the opportunity cost of buying from someone else. So, let's make their investment worth it.

It's also important to look at the stats around retaining customers. According to Bain & Company (2023), a study done across multiple brands has shown that a 5 per cent increase in retention correlates with at least a 25 per cent increase in profit.

Not only do repeat customers buy your products more, but they also have a higher AOV than first-time consumers. The number of previous purchases made and how long a customer has used your services directly impact how much a repeat customer spends in your business.

While the funnel encourages people to make their first sale, it is your repeat customers (and your retention marketing) that will create a sustainable business. Let's get into all the best ways to retain your customers.

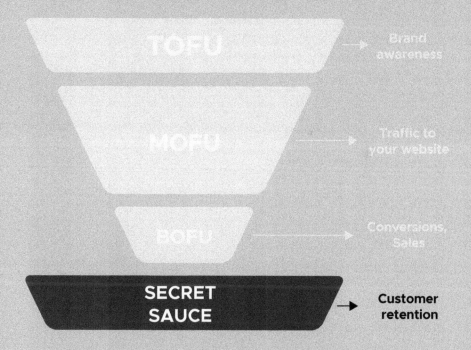

CHAPTER 21

Retention strategy #1: How to create an exceptional customer experience

Customer experience is more important than any paid marketing activity.

I want you to stop thinking of the customer experience as an operational function of your business, and start thinking of it as a marketing function. Parts of your business, such as customer service, dispatch times, and your returns process, are actually more important than any advertising or social media content. Yet, we don't focus on them every day because we think of them as operational in nature.

Imagine if every single customer touchpoint created an exceptional experience for your customers where they were made to feel important, all their questions were answered immediately and their objections were satisfyingly handled. This is what I want you to focus on when it comes to repeat purchases.

To create an exceptional experience, we are going to focus on three elements of your business: customer service touchpoints, dispatch and delivery, and returns and exchanges.

Customer service touchpoints

Geedup Co, one of my favourite clothing brands, uses customer service as its main marketing function, above paid ads, email marketing and SEO. I once heard the co-founder, Jake Paco, speak on stage about how they talk to their customers on social media. On their Instagram account, they get hundreds of messages per day (sometimes thousands when they launch a new collection). Their team not only reply to every single message, but they reply with voice notes and video messages and develop relationships with each person. The team is acutely aware of their raving fans and know them by name. They even go so far as to reserve stock for certain customers who they know are loyal.

That level of customer service is not common. As business owners, we quickly answer messages on our channels, but don't focus on it as a marketing tool. This creates a huge opportunity to increase repeat purchasers and brand advocates.

When I heard Jake speak about how much emphasis they place on customer communication, it was a big 'aha' moment for me. Customer retention starts with great communication. It led me to do a deep dive into how to make customer communication seamless. Here are my biggest tips:

♦ Make a list of every customer touchpoint in your business. This includes email, live chat, phone calls, Instagram DMs, Meta ads comments and Facebook messages.

- Allocate one week per touchpoint to focus on and improve it.

- Every week, look at that customer touchpoint and brainstorm ways to significantly improve the experience for the customer. Does it require a faster response time? Does it need a more personalised experience? Can you send videos instead of text replies? Can you add in automated FAQs?

- By the end of the exercise, your customers' experience from pre-purchase to post-purchase will outperform your competitors' and help keep your customers loyal.

Dispatch and delivery

A huge part of the customer experience is your dispatch and delivery time.

As an avid online shopper, there are certain websites I gravitate towards because of how fast their shipping is. Showpo is one of those websites. When I have an event to go to or if I'm speaking on stage, I have a pretty bad habit of waiting until the last minute to buy an outfit. I know, however, that there are websites like Showpo that can deliver an outfit to me the same day. So, rather than Googling any other stores, I go straight to Showpo.

Even if it doesn't have the exact dress I'm looking for, I would much rather have fast shipping. And that is a huge advantage for Showpo. They have made their dispatch and delivery timeframe one of their biggest competitive advantages. When I have shopped with them, they have never been delayed with their dispatch, and I trust that when I shop there in the future, their quick delivery time will be guaranteed. It is an incredible way to encourage customers to return.

Whether you use a third-party logistics (3PL), have your own warehouse or ship products from home, your dispatch time is

RETENTION

205

critical to having positive brand sentiment. Of course, if you have a product that takes time to make or create, then a fast dispatch time is not relevant. However, you need to make it abundantly clear on your website and in your FAQs what the timeframe is for dispatch and delivery.

If you are using a 3PL, you should be establishing key performance indicators (KPIs). Discuss same-day dispatch with them and see if it's possible and until what time of the day. You must also discuss how they handle peak-season dispatch. When we used a 3PL for Hero Packaging, they would ship out our orders the next business day, but when we had a big influx of sales, they would sometimes take four to five days to ship our orders. This caused a lot of frustration for our customers — and us because we had no control over it!

If you ship your own orders, then the faster the better. Some business owners are busy during the day — maybe they're studying or have a nine-to-five job — so they let orders come in and pack them on one day of the week to save time. This, in my opinion, is a mistake. You will notice that many of your one- and two-star reviews will be because an order wasn't received quickly enough. Remember, simply receiving the product they ordered is never enough for a great customer experience: shipping time is almost as important. Focus on speed and communication. So, even if you're just starting out and receiving a small number of orders a day, you should still focus on shipping your orders quickly, because this is arguably more important when you start your business, and you really need as many customers as possible coming back.

Returns and exchanges

According to Forrester (2023), the average return rate of clothing purchased online is 30 per cent, and KPMG found that up to 50 per cent may be the norm for clothing retailers following the holiday period.

That means that for every 100 orders that a fashion retailer makes, anywhere between 30 and 50 orders are returned.

When a customer decides to return a product, they expect one of three things: a refund, a store credit or an exchange. Having a comprehensive returns policy is critical to building trust, especially as a small business. In fact, according to Narvar (2023), 49 per cent of consumers actively check a retailer's returns policy before deciding to make a purchase, and over 30 per cent will not shop with a retailer who does not have a clear policy.

While I always advise businesses to offer all three options, there are many brands that do not offer refunds. White Fox Boutique is one of Australia's largest fast-fashion retailers. They sell millions of items of clothing every year, but they do not offer refunds for most returns; they only offer store credits or exchanges.

You may think: 'Well, if they are a fast-growing company, then maybe it's smart to not offer a refund on returns. If they can get away with it, so can I.' But there is a huge problem with this strategy — it significantly reduces customer retention. As a small business, the benefit of having a good refund policy far outweighs not having one.

By not having a refund policy, businesses can see a decrease in repeat purchasers and a negative effect on brand sentiment. According to Pro Carrier (2023), nearly 50 per cent of consumers won't return to a store that doesn't offer returns. On the other hand, 92 per cent of consumers interviewed said that they would return to a retailer that had a great refund and returns policy.

As business owners, we do not always have the luxury of only focusing on new customers — it is a very expensive exercise. Instead of looking at refunds as a negative element of the business, start looking at it as a way to increase customer happiness and trust. It is a powerful tool to get people to return to your store over and over again.

RETENTION

Retention strategy #2: How to use email marketing to bring customers back to your store

In my early eBay days, before I had a website, I knew that I wanted my competitive advantage to be my customer service. I had read hundreds of reviews online about my competitors, and the one thing that stood out to me was that customers said they had terrible customer service. In fact, the only way to communicate with those brands was through a form on their websites. I decided to create an exceptional customer service experience by answering all questions within an hour.

The only way I could communicate with my customers was through eBay messages (sellers don't have access to email addresses), so from the beginning, whenever someone made a purchase on my eBay store, I would message them the next day. The message would say something like this:

Hi!

My name is Anaita and I'm the owner of this business. I am so grateful that you have purchased from me. I will be shipping your bag today!

I would love to know if you have any questions.

Kind regards,

Anaita

I sent this message to every single person who purchased from me.

I tried to remember each and every eBay username that bought from me, and if I saw a name I recognised who bought from me again, I would send another message, and it read something like this:

Hi [Name]!

Wow, thank you so much for buying from me again. It makes me so happy to see you return to the store.

Is this a gift by any chance? I'd be happy to gift wrap it for you.

If you have any questions, please let me know.

Kind regards,

Anaita

These eBay messages were the best things I did in my business at the start. I had a 95 per cent response rate to my messages, and was able to generate return customers incredibly fast. In fact, the Small

Business Team at eBay reached out to feature me on their homepage. They were impressed with the level of growth I was having on their platform, and even invited me to their offices in Sydney to talk about how small businesses can thrive on eBay. It all came down to those post-purchase emails.

In those times, I had to send them manually, but now with email platforms, that same level of customer care can be automated through email flows. To this day, I still use those same emails with Hero Packaging to drive repeat purchases and positive brand sentiment.

Post-purchase email flows

Let's go through the flows you should set up for a great post-purchase experience.

Thank you for your purchase flow

This is very similar to the message I sent to customers on eBay. You want to thank them for choosing your business. Remember that it's not just that they bought from you; they spent their time and energy looking at options and ultimately bought from you over your competition.

As they have now made a purchase, they are dropped into your post-purchase email flow. In a post-purchase flow, there are transactional emails and marketing emails.

Emails such as the order confirmation and shipping information should automatically be sent to the customer — these are transactional emails and should be free of marketing activity.

The emails I'm going through in this section are marketing emails; these are less about the order and more about building a relationship with the customer. There are three emails that you can include in this flow:

1. Thank you (for new customers)

2. Thank you (for returning customers)

3. Instructional email

Trigger: Someone makes a purchase.

The wait time: One day after purchase.

EMAIL 1: MESSAGING FOR NEW CUSTOMERS

The messaging: For new customers, I recommend a plain text email. A simple thank you from you, the founder, works very well. You can include a little bit of your brand story and your mission, but the best policy is to keep it simple.

Optional: You can tell your new customers about your social platforms or a community they can join.

EMAIL 2: MESSAGING FOR REPEAT CUSTOMERS

The messaging: This is the email where you thank them for their continued support. The key here is to bring your brand personality into the email (e.g., professional, thoughtful, nurturing, playful, or witty). The email itself should be short and sweet, but should acknowledge that they have bought from you again. Write it as the founder and use first person.

The CTA for these emails is to ask them to send through any questions or queries about their order. The goal is to receive replies to your email, which you then reply to manually. The automated email is there to trigger a conversation with your customers.

EMAIL 3: INSTRUCTIONS

Trigger: The order has been fulfilled.

The wait time: Five days after shipping.

The messaging: Most items require some type of instruction, whether it's a guide on how to put it together or care instructions. This is a good chance to explain your product further.

This type of onboarding email helps cut down on customer service inquiries and reduces poor product adoption. The main benefit is that customers feel like they are supported in their purchase, and know that they can reply and ask any questions.

This email doesn't need to be from the founder. It could be a business email with icons, instructions and guides.

> **Tip**
>
> As long as there isn't any sales or marketing content in this series, you can get it tagged as a transactional email. This way, *all* customers are eligible to receive this important messaging—not just the ones who've opted in to email marketing.

RETENTION

Product review email flow

This is one of the most important emails you can send. Customers can give you a star rating, a comment and sometimes even a photo of them using the product. As you know, the more reviews you have, the more trustworthy your brand appears to new website visitors.

You can use your email platform for reviews (if they provide that service) or you can use a third-party reviews plugin for your website. I use an app called Judge.me, and this is where I send review emails from. They are both set up in a very similar way.

Trigger: When someone places an order.

The wait time: Fourteen days after purchase (you want to make sure the reviews email is sent after the customer has received the item and has had a couple of days to use it or test it).

The messaging: This is less of a marketing email and more of a transactional email, so it's best to keep it short and to the point. The messaging should be along the lines of:

◆ We would love to get your feedback.

◆ Please leave an honest review of our products.

◆ This is very helpful for others to learn about our brand and products.

Again, the content of the email is asking someone to review the product they bought, but you need to add in your brand personality. This includes the subject line; here are some examples of subject lines:

◆ So … did you like it?

◆ Are you impressed?

◆ Re: Your purchase.

◆ Quick order check in.

◆ Would love your thoughts.

Replenishment email flow

This email flow is for brands who have products that are bought repeatedly within a certain timeframe; for example, toothpaste, shower filters, hairspray, packaging, batteries, women's sanitary items. These emails are a great reminder for customers to repurchase the product.

This is all about timing. You need to analyse your customer data to see what the average time is between purchases and then send the email just before their product is scheduled to run out.

Trigger: When someone places an order.

The wait time: This depends on the usage time of your product (if applicable). For example, skincare may be 60 days, while food seasoning might be 30 days. Set the time just before customers usually replenish.

The messaging: This is a chance to show your personality! If you are an accounting firm, you may need to be more professional when reminding a client to lodge their tax return. But for other businesses, you can make this email fun and casual.

Take the brand Who Gives a Crap, for example. In their replenishment email, they have a flow chart that starts with the question 'Do you have a bum?' It goes on to ask a series of questions with 'yes' or 'no' answers, which ultimately leads someone to the end of the flowchart where it says: Buy some toilet paper.

It is a hilarious way to remind people to place their next order without being too pushy. Here are some great subject lines you can use:

◆ I think it's time ...

◆ Need a top up?

RETENTION

- ◆ Oops, did your [product] just run out?

- ◆ Don't you hate it when this happens?

Back-in-stock flow

Implementing a back-in-stock journey will prompt your customers to sign up for an alert when a specific item is back in stock. You can then make these customers feel special by contacting them first when the item becomes available. This is best done through a third-party plugin or app, such as Notify Me: Back in Stock on Shopify.

Trigger: When you add inventory/stock to the back end of your website for a particular product.

The wait time: Immediately after restocking.

The messaging: This is a simple email that will have a link to the back-in-stock product. You can use copy, such as 'Look what's back in stock!' or 'Did you miss me? I'm back.'

There should be no other CTA other than pushing people to the product page to purchase that product.

Email campaigns

Once your flows have been set up, there are email campaigns that you can send to further build your connection with the customer, and to also encourage them to purchase again. These emails should be sent about once a week.

When sending email campaigns to customers, your goal is to get them to return and make another purchase. But the best part of sending email campaigns in this section of the funnel is that they have already bought from you before and are, therefore, easier to convert into a sale.

We don't need to always sell, sell, sell. While some campaigns will encourage customers to repurchase, there are also a number of ways to speak to them in a helpful way. Here are some ideas for email campaigns:

◆ cross-sells and upsells

◆ product hacks

◆ staff picks

◆ repeat purchase incentives.

Cross-sells and upsells

These emails are a fantastic way to encourage repeat purchases. Using your website data, you can see which two products are commonly bought together, and then you can filter your email subscribers by those who have bought one of those products (and not bought the other), and send them an email about the product that other customers commonly buy. You can do this for most of your products. By using your data, these emails will get a higher conversion rate. Example subject lines include:

◆ Based on our data, we know you will love this.

◆ You need this in your life.

◆ Customers like you also bought this.

◆ Over 300 customers love this one thing.

◆ This is a must-have for your collection.

◆ You bought that, now get this.

RETENTION

Product hacks

This email is a great way to show customers how to use products in multiple ways. Let's say someone bought a black one-piece swimsuit on your site. You could send them an email about how all your one-pieces can double as a luxe top when paired with high waisted pants. You can show examples of someone wearing a swimsuit to the pool and then wearing it on a date night, and you can showcase multiple colours. This product hack email not only shows the customer how to use their current purchase, but also encourages them to buy more in different colours.

Product hacks can be funny and a bit quirky too. A couple of years ago, I sent an email to our Hero Packaging customers telling them not to buy Christmas gift-wrapping and to use their Hero Packaging mailers instead. We wrapped all our presents in our Hero Packaging mailers and took photos of us opening gifts. The email was a huge success with customers sending us photos of their Christmas trees with Hero Packaging mailers as wrapping underneath. Customers started sharing their photos on social media, and we received many new eyeballs and followers.

Here are some subject lines you could use:

- Here's something you didn't know.

- I bet you didn't know you could do this with [product].

- Prepare to be amazed.

- This is one of the coolest things about [product].

- Our [product] is actually a [hack]?!

- It's not what you think it is.

Staff picks

You know when you walk into a bookstore and you go to your favourite section and there are signs under some books that say 'staff pick'? You automatically want to learn more about those books because they come from a recommendation.

This is the same idea for the email: talk about products that are your staff's favourites. If it's only you in the business, then talk about your favourites. It's such a great way to show off other products in your range. Example subject lines include:

- Staff picks you'll love.

- These are highly recommended by our team.

- [Staff member's name] loves this, so you know it's good.

- Have a look at what our team are using.

- Founder's top picks.

- Here's what I recommend as the founder.

Repeat purchase incentives

When someone buys from you and hasn't returned to your store, you can give them a little push by incentivising their next purchase. This can be done through a personalised discount or through a gift with purchase.

I prefer to incentivise with a gift rather than a discount because you are not losing any margin with the purchase, and you can offer a very low-cost item as the gift. Let's say you sell kids clothes, and your AOV is $120. Rather than giving a 20 per cent discount for the next purchase, you could offer a free limited-edition detangling brush.

RETENTION

219

The 20 per cent discount costs you $24, whereas the brush would probably cost you about $1 to $2, and has a high perceived value to the customer.

In order for this to work, you need to list the gift on your website as a product and in the email with a specific code for your customer to get the brush for free. Here are some subject lines that work for this email campaign:

- Here's a free [product].

- Free [gift] for the next 24 hours.

- I want to gift you something.

- Take 20 per cent off your next purchase.

- 20 per cent off for 24 hours only.

- Here's a gift to say thank you.

CHAPTER 23

Retention strategy #3: How to use Meta ads to retarget your customers

When I analyse the Facebook ads accounts of clients, there is always one thing in common: their retargeting ads have the highest return on ads spend (ROAS) compared with all their other campaigns.

This is because this campaign is targeting people who have purchased from their store within the last six months, but who have not purchased again in the last month. If your product can be bought every few months, then this campaign will be your winning campaign!

The objective: Sales/conversions.

The type of campaign: Manual.

Budget: The budget for this can be lower than other campaigns as the pool of people you are targeting is smaller (i.e., people who have bought from you in the last six months). A starting budget could be $10 per day, depending on how large the specific audience is. If you are just starting, Meta may deem this audience too small, so you will need to wait until you have more customers in this pool.

Audience: You will be targeting people who have purchased your product. These are people who have purchased from you within the last six months (180 days) but who have *not* purchased within the last month (30 days).

In order to target them, you need to create these audiences in the 'Audience' tab in your Meta ads. Let's continue and create the following audiences:

- ◆ Custom audience: Website purchasers in the last 180 days.

- ◆ Custom audience: Website purchasers in the last 30 days (you will be excluding this audience).

Ad creative

The best type of ad for this campaign is a dynamic collections ad, where Meta will show certain products to the audience based on their previous behaviour on your website.

A collections ad typically has an image or video as the main ad creative, with four to six products (with product information) displayed underneath. These products can change depending on the person who is seeing the ad. Here are some examples of images or videos you can use in this campaign:

- Collage: A collection of all your best-selling products or a video displaying each one.

- New product drops: A video of a new product or collection.

- Seasonal visuals: Using key gifting periods or seasons to showcase how your product can be used at that time.

- Lifestyle videos: Choose a video of your product in use; this could be a user-generated video or a video of you showing how to use the product.

Copy

The copy should acknowledge that they have bought from you before. Here are some examples of copy you could use:

- Running out of [product name]?

- Need more of [product name]?

- You may not have seen our last collection drop.

- We miss you!

- We know you will love this!

Your retargeting ad campaign is done! Keep an eye on the results because this one should give you great returns. Allow it to run for at least 30 days before you make any significant changes.

RETENTION

PART IV
The magic bucket

Having repeat customers is incredible, but having loyal customers, raving fans and brand advocates is magical. These customers are in your magic bucket. All businesses should aim to consistently fill their magic bucket with these loyal customers who adore their brand. Loyalty and advocacy start and end with great customer experiences. From pre-purchase to post-purchase, the experience a customer has with your store is the foundation to creating loyalty. Once they have had a good experience, you can leverage this to make them even happier by implementing strategies that continuously surprise and delight them.

Creating loyal customers in your business is one of the cheapest ways to earn recurring revenue and build a community of raving fans.

I am about to tell you a loyalty stat that may surprise you. According to Exploding Topics (2024), price is the number one factor keeping customers loyal to their favourite brands. When I first heard this, I was surprised because I have brands that I am loyal to where price has no bearing on my decision. But the more I thought about it, the more I realised that many brands consciously focus on price competitiveness because they have not figured out how to make customers loyal based on human and emotional connection, purpose and mission, and community. Major brands, such as Amazon, Walmart, Costco and Target, retain loyalty because they can provide the cheapest goods. However, as small businesses, where maintaining the lowest price is difficult, we need to encourage loyalty by providing an exceptional purchasing experience, making customers feel like they are part of a community or movement, forging emotional connections, and rewarding them for returning to your brand over and over again.

There are the four key ways to do exactly that.

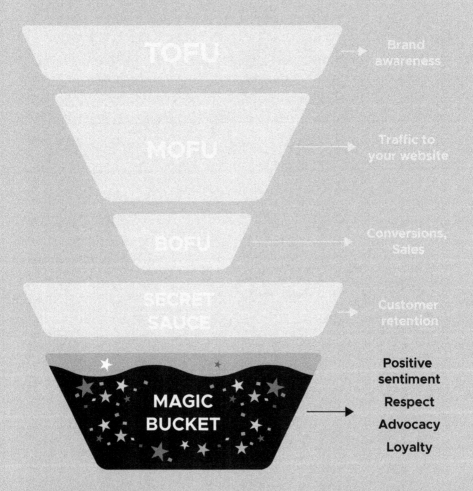

CHAPTER 24

Magic bucket strategy #1: Creating a loyalty program that works

I love makeup. Even if I'm not leaving the house or meeting anyone, I always put makeup on. It makes me feel like I'm ready for the day and subconsciously makes me feel like I can tackle anything. I have a core selection of makeup products that I use and purchase over and over again. And even though I could buy them from many online stores, I only shop at Mecca. I don't care if there is a sale on another website, I am loyal to Mecca and it is all because of its loyalty program.

Every quarter, Mecca rewards its customers with its loyalty program, Beauty Loop. Customers are rewarded with a box of free samples. The size (travel size to full size) and brands of the samples depends on how much you spend. You are put into different levels ranging from level 1 to level 4 (the ultimate loyalty level).

I recently texted a friend telling her that I had hit level 3 and how excited I was to get my Beauty Loop box. It feels like a prize every quarter and the excitement of jumping up a level is unmatched by any other business loyalty programs.

Mecca's program has been built over a decade, and has had some of Australia's best marketing minds working on it. The logistics of a program like that are very complex. So, how can we, as small business owners, give our customers a similar experience?

A loyalty program in any business is a great way to incentivise customers to return to your store as it rewards a company's repeat customers with discounts and gifts.

With a loyalty program, businesses can offer points or benefits to customers. In return, customers redeem points for discounts, free products or insider perks. The goal is to incentivise them to continue buying from your business.

The payoff for having a loyalty and rewards program is huge. In fact, a 2023 survey by Statista found that 79 per cent of consumers indicated that loyalty programs affect their likelihood of continuing to buy from a brand. Another poll found that 80 per cent of people claim to purchase more regularly from a brand after signing up to its loyalty program. There are three types of loyalty programs.

1. Points-based loyalty programs

Points programs are the most common type of rewards programs. They let customers accumulate reward points they can redeem for freebies, cash back, perks and so on. Rewards customers don't just earn points from purchases; they can also earn loyalty points by posting about your products on social media and tagging your brand, leaving reviews or celebrating a milestone, such as a birthday.

How it works:

- You will need a loyalty app for your website. I use Smile.io but there are many on the market.

- You need to establish the rules; for example, how many points does a customer receive for every $1 spent, and consequently, how many points do they need to earn store credit or a gift.

- Determine whether customers can earn more points by completing various tasks, such as referring a friend to your store, sharing their order on social media or simply celebrating their birthday. You can allocate a number of points, and they will automatically receive those points when they complete one of those activities.

- Make sure your customers know about your loyalty program. You can talk about it through emails and social media, and include information on your website.

The best part is that it is all automated.

2. Tiered loyalty programs

Tiered customer loyalty programs are a type of membership where customers get different benefits depending on their spend or the number of orders they place. These customer reward programs give customers a goal. The higher their tier, the more exclusive and better the rewards they'll receive.

This is the type of loyalty program that Mecca uses, where it offers different sample boxes to customers with different spends. It has truly perfected the program and created incredibly loyal fans.

So, what has Mecca done so right?

- ◆ Made the process of signing up easy: When you purchase, whether it's in store or online, you can sign up quickly by providing your name, email address and phone number. On the website, this is done via a simple check box.

- ◆ Doesn't go on sale very often: This is a pretty rare thing in online retail. Mecca rarely has a sale, but instead focuses on its rewards. This not only means that it retains a great profit margin, but customers actually want to spend more because of the perks they receive.

- ◆ Rewards are worth it: Mecca doesn't gift cheap products. All the products in its Beauty Loop program are trending, hyped-up and viral products that customers are dying to try.

- ◆ Shout it from the rooftops: If you have ever bought from Mecca or visited its website, it's hard to avoid their Beauty Loop messaging. This is the main marketing strategy and it's made clear from its Google Ads to the in-store experience.

- ◆ Have a platform for loyalists to chat: A few years ago, Mecca created an exclusive Facebook group called Mecca Chit Chat where fans of Mecca could talk about their Beauty Loop boxes and their makeup in general. It has grown to over 200 000 members. This platform gives customers a place to ask questions and feel like they can share their love for Mecca products with others.

3. Paid loyalty programs

Adairs, a leading homewares store, has a popular paid loyalty program called Linen Lovers. This costs customers $19.95 for two years, but in return, they get a permanent discount on all items in store among other benefits. This program is so successful that in 2023, Adairs said that 83 per cent of its sales came from Linen Lovers members.

Paid or fee-based loyalty programs give customers immediate and ongoing benefits for a participation fee. These fees can be recurring or one off. There are many brands with paid loyalty programs, including Amazon with Amazon Prime and Kogan with Kogan First.

The reason it works is because of the win-win model: you as the business owner benefit from recurring revenue and customer loyalty, and customers benefit from ongoing discounts that are worth more than the membership fee.

Paid loyalty programs can be more incentivising than standard free loyalty programs. McKinsey's research found that 59 per cent of paid-program customers were more likely to choose that brand over the competition. They were also 43 per cent more likely to buy from that brand on a more frequent basis. How you can do it:

- ◆ Most loyalty programs allow you to add a paid membership. Some popular apps include Smile.io, Stamped.io and Loyalty Lion.

- ◆ Make sure that the rewards within the paid membership are worth the yearly spend.

- ◆ Continue to surprise and delight those members to keep them engaged and happy. You can do this by giving them early access to sales and new products, adding unexpected gifts with their purchases and sending them personal thank you emails from you as the founder.

- ◆ Ask customers what they would like to receive in this program. You can do this using a post-purchase email for customers who have bought from you two or more times or at the bottom of email campaigns. You can get customers to simply reply to the email or direct them to a feedback form.

◆ Make the program known to your visitors and customers, and encourage signups on product pages, in the cart and also through email and social content.

CHAPTER 25

Magic bucket strategy #2: Giving your customers a place to chat

One of the best ways to foster loyalty is giving your customers a platform to gather and discuss your brand. Girls Get Off is a sexual wellness brand that sells sex toys, and it has formed an incredible community of women who want to learn and talk about sexual wellness. When the founders recognised that these women craved other women to talk to, they created a Facebook group called Girls Get Off Uncensored. They started to tell their customers about it through emails and social media, and within a couple of years, they had over 37 000 members join the group.

While the group is brand led, the conversations are not just about the brand. There are posts offering advice, stories and experiences, and it gives women a safe space to share their thoughts. Girls Get Off is able to leverage this platform to not only talk intimately with their customers, but they can also talk about new product launches, offer a sale and give brand updates.

The question is, can you do this for your business?

Not every business has a product that lends itself to community forums, but if you have a brand or product in an industry that people are always asking questions about, telling stories about, recommending products or sharing experiences, then it would work well.

To get started, you first need to choose the platform you want to use, such as Facebook groups, Patreon or Discord. Name the group something to do with your brand name and create the rules and entry requirements. For Girls Get Off, they ask for an email address, the gender you identify with and whether you have read the terms and conditions.

Once the group has been created, it's time to start inviting customers and social media followers to join. Initially, you need to lead the discussion and try to get as much engagement as possible. Whenever someone comments, make sure you reply quickly. The initial hype will come from you as the brand owner. Over time, customers will take over and start leading the conversations. It's important that you or someone from your business monitors the group chat every day to make sure the posts stay on topic and don't go rogue. This is a platform that needs quite a lot of management.

However, it is worth the work because it is another type of digital asset where you 'own' an audience and it can be just as powerful as email marketing.

CHAPTER 26

Magic bucket strategy #3: Giving your customers FOMO

When customers have a fear of missing out (FOMO) on a gift or being part of a new product drop, it creates a sense of loyalty. There is no company that creates better FOMO than Hi-Smile. When you follow Hi-Smile on social media or you visit their website or see an ad, there is always a feeling that they are creating something exciting. They show thousands of people using their products, they partner with brands and influencers and always have a freebie or discount running. It makes their audience want to participate and feel like they are part of the action.

Here are some of the ways that Hi-Smile creates a FOMO brand:

♦ Their website changes its offering frequently, so it's always fun to visit. Today, the offer might be a free toothpaste with any purchase; tomorrow, it might be a new product launch. It keeps the audience excited. If you want to create a fun website, a great way to do it is to change the offer, change the banner images or add new videos.

♦ The website also features time-sensitive deals. It often includes a countdown timer on the site to increase urgency. I always advise brands to run time-sensitive offers as authentic offers. If your website states that the deal will end at a certain time, make sure that it does end at that time. Make sure you don't only say it to get more purchases and then extend the time. This can be quite frustrating for customers, and you can lose trust.

♦ They partner with some of the most popular influencers on social media, such as Anna Paul, to co-create products. These new products are usually limited editions, so their audiences are keen to get their hands on them before they sell out.

This sense of FOMO is a powerful marketing tool, and it's done through surprising customers in different ways — and often. By constantly changing the offers and using new user-generated content, your audience will feel like your brand is fresh and exciting.

What I've realised about most brands is that they stay the same — they use the same marketing strategies, they rarely switch up their content, and they don't add new, exciting elements to their website. If you start to introduce FOMO elements to your marketing strategy, you will see an increase in customer sentiment and repurchase behaviour.

CHAPTER 27

Magic bucket strategy #4: Treating customers like VIPs

If you want customers to be loyal to you, you need to give them VIP service. They should have first access to sales and product launches; they also need to have exclusive content delivered to them — content that other subscribers and customers don't receive. When you do a gift with purchase, they may even receive a better gift than other customers.

Making customers feel like they are part of a very special group leads to a sense of belonging and that feeling of friendship with a brand. Here is how you can treat your loyal customers like VIPs:

◆ First, identify who you want to give a VIP service to: I like to choose customers who have bought from my business five or more times. Your VIP customers could depend on the type of product you sell.

- ◆ Segment these customers in your email platform and name the segment 'Loyal VIPs'.

- ◆ Send your customer list an email to let them know that they are on the VIP list, and they will get access to certain things before anyone else.

- ◆ The key is to let your other customers know about the VIP group. The goal is for everyone to want to be a part of it, and strive to spend more in your store so they can have priority access and privileges.

- ◆ When you are planning your product launches or making any announcements, consider having two distinct strategies: one that tells your VIP list first and one that announces it to the rest of your customers.

According to Exploding Topics (2024), 88 per cent of consumers say it takes three or more purchases to build brand loyalty. That means, by focusing on customer retention, and getting customers to purchase more than three times from you, you are building a solid community of loyal customers who, given the choice, will select your products above any other competitor. Those customers fall into your magic bucket and should be treated like royalty. Having loyalty strategies in place when you first start your business will help greatly in creating consistent sales in your business.

CHAPTER 28

Magic bucket strategy #5: Using email marketing to make customers feel special

Every year, on 5 November, I get a full body massage. I spend one hour on the massage table and the next hour drinking tea and having a delicious breakfast in the massage parlour's gardens. That yearly treat is a birthday gift from my local spa. Two weeks before my birthday, I always receive an email wishing me a happy birthday and an offer to get a massage at 50 per cent off. It's something I genuinely look forward to every birthday, and I always take up the offer. But I don't just go to that spa on my birthday — whenever I want to feel pampered, I book in a treatment at that spa. I do this for many reasons: the service is exceptional, but, more importantly, they actually remind me when

I haven't booked an appointment in a while. The emails they send look like they are from the spa owner and include all the details about my last massage. It feels personalised and I appreciate that.

Email marketing in this part of the customer journey is not about convincing someone to buy something for the first time — it's about making your customers feel seen and appreciated. By remembering something special in their lives, you are creating positive brand sentiment.

There is one email flow I want you to set up and three email campaigns I want you to include in your marketing plan.

Email flow: Celebration emails

Just like my local spa, I want you to celebrate your customers on days that are important to them. This could be a birthday, an anniversary, the first time they bought from you, their business anniversary or even their children's birthdays.

One of the best ways to collect data about this special date is either through the email collection popup or form or through your loyalty app. On your popup or form, you can simply add a field where they can add that special date and it will populate this in your email platform.

If you choose to gather this information through a loyalty app, you have the added benefit of offering them extra loyalty points automatically every year.

At Hero Packaging, our customers are business owners, so we use our loyalty app, Smile.io, to collect business anniversary dates, and every year, on that date, the app will automatically send an email and give them an extra 500 points. They can use these points, in addition to their current points, to receive a discount on their next purchase.

Even if you don't want to offer a discount or points, simply acknowledging that special day could make your customers feel seen and appreciated. Let's go through how to set up this flow in your email platform.

Trigger: Customer's birthday.

The wait time: None (the email should be sent on their birthday).

The messaging: The best gift from a brand is getting a product or service for free! It's the freebies that get customers returning to your store to claim them.

My tip here is to give them something for free with their next purchase. While we would all love to gift our customers things with nothing in return, profitability comes first. So, by customers returning to your store and purchasing something and getting a gift when they do so, it not only makes them feel like they are being celebrated, but you get a returning and paying customer.

As we talked about in Chapter 24, Mecca does this exceptionally well with its loyalty program, Beauty Loop. Depending on your loyalty level, you receive a special gift on your birthday. It could be free products or a makeup application. The clever thing that Mecca does here is to only give free makeup applications to those in the top two levels of their program — that is, the people who have spent over $1200 in the last year on Mecca products. So, while it is a freebie, it comes with a minimum spend.

The email that you send to customers to celebrate their special date should include a lot of your brand personality, whether that's a personal note from the founder or a birthday-themed, image-based email.

Make the gift clear, easily redeemable and include a time limit on it.

MAGIC BUCKET

Email campaigns

In November 2023, I sent an email to our most loyal customers that generated an 88 per cent open rate and 40 per cent click-through rate. I had used Shopify to generate a report on customers who had purchased from us 20 or more times within the last three years, and sent them a simple email to say thank you. This is what the email said:

Hi [name],

As the year is drawing to a close, I wanted to take a moment to say thank you for supporting Hero Packaging. I see that you have bought from us well over 20 times in the last few years and I'm incredibly grateful.

I want to let you know that you can email me personally any time if you ever have questions about Hero, our products or sustainability. My email is [my work email].

In one week, we are having a big sale, which I haven't announced to the public yet. I am giving you first access from now. Please use the code [discount code] to get 25 per cent off all packaging.

I would really appreciate it if you don't share the code with anyone as it's exclusively for you.

Hope you have a lovely week!

Anaita x

In our five years of operation, that email campaign resulted in one of our biggest days of sales ever. It also resulted in 30 per cent of the recipients replying to the email telling me how much they loved Hero Packaging.

Loyal customers will not only continue to shop with you, but they will feel a somewhat personal connection to you as well. That is pretty special.

There are a few ways to communicate with your loyal customers, but emails are the best way to provide a personalised approach to a group of people.

Here are some email ideas to send to your magic bucket.

Top 5 per cent

When was the last time someone told you that you were in the top 5 per cent of anything? It's a pretty nice feeling. Now, imagine telling your loyal customers that same thing. That would make them feel pretty special.

For this email campaign, I want you to identify who is in your top 5 per cent of customers. This could be calculated by total order amount or by the number of orders. The email will tell them that they are in your top 5 per cent of customers, and that they will receive extra benefits like early access to launches and sales, surprise gifts, and maybe even personal access to you, the founder.

If you are a small business with only a handful of people in your top 5 per cent, you can even email them manually and include more personalised information about their previous orders and what other products you personally recommend.

Something to think about: if a customer falls out of the top 5 per cent, they won't be included in future emails. This is because the top 5 per cent list of customers is exported from your email platform manually every time you run this type of campaign.

MAGIC BUCKET

Free points

A great sign of appreciation is surprising your best customers with free points. Using your loyalty program, you can delight your customers by gifting them 500, 1000 or 2000 points that are redeemable for store credit.

A handbag company in New York, Caraa, randomly surprises their most loyal customers with a 'points drop', where they put 1000 points into their loyalty program account. I love this because it's simple and easy to implement, and by using the loyalty app, you can personalise each email with their points balance.

Exclusive or early access

There is no better feeling as a customer than getting access to something before anyone else. Being in an exclusive group where the sale is a secret makes those customers feel important.

This email lets your customers know that they are VIPs and have early access (for a short time) or exclusive access (no one else will get this promotion). Early access emails work the best when the time between the VIP group email and the public email is one week or less. This puts a time limit on the VIP offering and persuades them to purchase before anyone else.

CHAPTER 29

Magic bucket strategy #6: Building a personal brand

In January 2021, five large boxes filled with books landed on my doorstep. This wasn't just any book, this was a book I had written, designed, and had printed over six months. I remember opening the door and feeling an enormous sense of overwhelm.

You see, the year before, during lockdown, I fell pregnant with my third daughter. At the same time, I had also decided to sell my first business and, to make things even harder, I decided I wanted to write a marketing book. Somewhere between running to the bathroom with morning sickness and negotiating the business sale with multiple buyers, I wrote a 40 000-word book within three months. I found a fantastic designer and illustrator who put the finishing touches on the book, and after another three months, the book was ready to be printed.

However, in the same week that it went to print, my business got sold and I was a week away from having the baby. It was incredibly busy. I was exhausted and I wasn't able to appreciate each achievement.

So, when those 500 books landed on my front doorstep, I stood there looking at the boxes, overwhelmed and unable to process what to do.

I had been so busy writing it, selling a business and giving birth that I actually hadn't figured out a way to sell the books. What's even worse is that I had no one to sell them to because my Instagram business account had been sold to the new owners of my business, and all those followers were no longer mine.

I carried each of the boxes inside, plonked them down in my home office, and sat down to figure out what to do. Instinctively, I opened up my favourite app — a somewhat new social media app called TikTok — that I had been scrolling through during my downtime. As luck would have it, the first video that showed up was a girl talking to camera about being fired from her job and starting a business and loving it. Her video had 20000 views at that point, and in the comments, people were offering to hire her services.

It was in that moment I knew I had to start creating content on TikTok. If I wanted to sell my book and get awareness for the book from around the world, TikTok was the place to do it. So, I set up a creator account and I challenged myself to create at least three videos a day, seven days a week. And that's exactly what I did. Every day, I'd open up my book to a random page, find a marketing tip and read it to the camera.

Fast forward three months, after creating multiple videos a day about marketing tips, I had grown my followers from 0 to 70000 people, and I had sold over a thousand books, even before my book launch event.

As my followers grew, unexpected opportunities started to present themselves.

Brands started reaching out to me to pay me to create videos for them. Podcasters reached out to me to speak on their business podcasts. Business groups reached out to me to speak on panels. These were things I never saw coming, but I loved it. In fact, I loved these opportunities so much, I started to film BTS footage of them and post them to TikTok. And, as other brands saw what I was doing, more and more enquiries flooded in.

My mentality was: say 'yes' and think about it later because you never know if this opportunity will come again, and you never know what it will lead to.

I am happy that I said 'yes' every time because it led to many unexpected, goal-achieving, money-making and profile-building opportunities. Not to mention it helped to boost brand awareness for Hero Packaging.

Building a personal brand has allowed me to combine the two things that I love: e-commerce and teaching. It has given me the opportunity to teach on stage, on podcasts, on panels, in masterclasses, in masterminds and on one-on-one calls.

Based on three years of building my personal brand, here are my five key learnings that I want to share with you.

1. Know where you want to go

Trevor Noah once asked Oprah Winfrey what she would say is the one common characteristic that gets people to where they want to go.

She replied, 'People get to where they want to go because they know where they want to go. The question people should ask themselves is "what do I really want?"'

MAGIC BUCKET

When you are building a personal brand and increasing your followers, you need to know why you want to do that. What is your purpose or your mission? Do you want to build another income stream? Do you genuinely enjoy speaking on stage? Do you want to start a coaching business? Do you want to help as many people as possible?

Knowing your goals is the first step to reaching them. When it comes to building a personal brand, it's easy to get lost in the follower growth and engagement. You want to set clear goals so you know which opportunities to look out for.

2. Build out your channels

One of the most important things you should do when creating a personal brand is treat it like a business. The product is your skills, and you need to sell them. Here are some steps to take when starting a personal brand:

- Think carefully about your name: Do you want your personal brand to be under your name or a pseudonym? Mine is 'Sell Anything Online'. Whatever name you choose, keep it consistent on all platforms.

- Set up a simple website with your bio, 'layers' (more on this next), services and awards that you've won.

- Set up all social media handles, including TikTok, Instagram, Facebook, Twitter and LinkedIn. Even if you aren't using them right now, you want to own your brand name on those channels for future use.

- Pick two channels to start on: one that you're comfortable with and one that puts you outside of your comfort zone. The latter is about testing and experimenting with a new platform and audience.

3. Apply the layering method

'What's your genius zone?'

This was a question I received from a colleague during a marketing conference.

When I asked her to explain, she said: 'Well, if you are mentoring business owners and speaking on stage, you must have a genius zone — a topic you specialise in.'

I was a little embarrassed to say that I didn't have one main genius zone. In fact, I loved speaking about a variety of topics, but had no specialty.

I thought about that question a lot, and the more I thought about it, the more I disagreed with it. Having a genius zone pigeonholes you into one or two topics. However, your knowledge is multi-faceted and comes from a variety of lived experiences. Your ability to grow your personal brand is not just based on one topic; it comes from your personal story, your business journey and topics that you have expertise in. This is what I like to call the 'layering method'.

The idea of the layering method is that every single person has a collection of lived experiences in their personal and business life. Many of those experiences are directly related to where they are today and affect their behaviour, their achievements and their goals. The experiences you have had and the goals you tried to achieve, by default, make you an expert on them — whether you failed or succeeded, you have lessons that are worth sharing.

These experiences, or 'layers', are the foundations of your personal brand. They are the reasons why someone will ask you to speak or be

MAGIC BUCKET

interviewed. To use the layering method, there are five things I want you to take note of:

1. Write down the big experiences in your personal life. Mine have been coming to Australia as an immigrant, not fitting in at school because of my culture, having three children, and choosing the right partner to be in business with and raise kids with.

2. Now write down the big experiences in your business life. Mine have been quitting multiple jobs, starting a business that copied another business, starting my second business, scaling a B2B e-commerce business, scaling a sustainability-focused business, growing too fast, making huge financial mistakes, writing a book and building a personal brand.

3. Write down the topics you love to talk about. Mine are digital marketing, business trends, growing small businesses and growth mindsets.

4. Write down the things that have helped you over time (e.g., quotes, certain people, rituals, and tools).

5. Write down the goals you want to achieve.

All of these layers are your points of expertise.

Now I want you to start creating content around these layers. Talk about each of them and talk about them often.

A lot of this content should sit across your social media accounts, your personal brand website and your bio on LinkedIn. Make it known that these are topics you can speak on, so that anyone who is looking for a speaker or panellist with your experience can find you.

4. Be over prepared

In July 2023, I was on Mark Bouris's podcast, *The Mentor*. I had followed Mark for over ten years and being on his podcast was a big goal of mine. Jess, his producer, had emailed me a list of questions prior to the interview, but in her email she also said: 'He goes off-script, so be prepared for anything.'

Little did she know that I over prepare for any speaking engagement I'm given. This is because I'm not a natural speaker. I still think of myself as a shy Indian girl with an accent who shakes when she needs to speak to more than two people at a time. So, in order to appear confident, I prepare more than I need to. For that particular interview, I:

◆ wrote out all the questions she provided and wrote down my answers for them.

◆ wrote out other potential questions about my business I thought he could ask, and I practised my answers.

◆ listened to ten of his previous podcast interviews and every time he asked a question, I paused it and answered the question as though he had just asked me.

◆ read one of his books and made a note of a few questions I wanted to ask him.

◆ read through as many news articles about him as I could and memorised as much of his Wikipedia page as possible.

Do I think I went overboard with my preparation? Absolutely not. I knew, walking into that interview, there was nothing he could ask me that I hadn't practised for. I walked in nervous, but I walked in ready.

Being over prepared means that nothing will catch you off guard. If you are a bit more introverted, like me, then over preparedness will give you the confidence for any opportunity. But don't mistake this for perfectionism — I'm not asking you to memorise your answers word for word. I'm asking you to do your research and educate yourself in-depth on the topic you're speaking about and who you are speaking with.

5. Stop talking about yourself

Richard Branson once said: 'Ego has no place when it comes to public speaking. The best speakers, like the best leaders, know that they are there to serve.'

I have listened to hundreds of speakers, and one of the main differentiators between a bad speaker and a great speaker is their ability to relate their story to the audience.

A bad speaker that I listened to recently started off with an intriguing introduction. She spoke about challenges she faced in her previous business and with her previous relationship and how she managed to get through that time. However, 30 minutes into it, the talk had not progressed. She was still talking about her personal situation and had not related it to the audience at all. After 55 minutes, she summed up her presentation and gave the audience one business tip. But by that stage, many people had switched off and were either checking their phones or packing up.

People usually follow others online or listen to speeches, podcasts and panel discussions because they assume they are going to get something from their content to improve their lives. So, when that doesn't happen, those same people disengage.

Saying something like 'what I want you to take away from this is …' is much better than 'I did this and I learnt from it'.

If you want to build an audience and speak to them in a way that engages them, you must learn how to tell your story but make it about them.

Flex Mami: Becoming an icon

Lillian Ahenkan, also known as Flex Mami, is a best-selling author, TV presenter, podcaster, DJ, media influencer, social commentator, speaker, model, TV Week Logie nominee, founder and CEO. To put it simply, Flex Mami gets paid to be herself. Recognised internationally as a digital and cultural icon, she creates and facilitates challenging, nourishing conversations, and cultivates communities through social media.

With a platform focused on legacy, intention and reprioritising people, Flex's superpower is cultivating dialogue and encouraging her community to think critically about themselves and the world around them.

Named Instagram Australia's #YoungEntrepreneur 2020, Flex is the founder and CEO of the company behind the conversation card game ReFlex, and jewellery brand Post Primadonna. Here, we get to the core of what makes Flex Mami so unique and why it 'works'.

The genesis of Flex Mami

Flex Mami's journey began with her initial foray into DJing, which she describes as the pivotal element in shaping her personal brand. While working as a publicist at a PR agency, she found herself feeling disillusioned with the industry.

In an effort to seek fulfilment elsewhere, she took on a role as a door girl in Kings Cross, an area in Sydney renowned for its nightlife. When an opportunity to DJ for the club came up, she asked the bar manager if she could use the DJ equipment to learn on and practice with during the day. This opportunity marked the beginning of her dual role as a DJ and door girl, a combination she initially did not regard as a 'real job'.

However, her perspective shifted dramatically as her DJ gigs became more frequent. From a single two-hour slot on a Friday night, she quickly progressed to performing 25 hours a week, all while maintaining her full-time job in PR. This rapid escalation in her DJ career ten years ago was the start of her incredibly successful personal brand.

Shooting her shot

Within 12 months of starting her DJ career, Flex became an MTV presenter thanks to one simple action. A freelance producer wanted to feature her in a video editorial about the 'It Girls of Sydney'. When the profile fell through, Flex asked for the direct contact at MTV. 'Because I was nurtured by PR girlies, I had a very bulldog PR mindset. Like, send the press release, reach out, build the relationship. So, I really don't think I would have thought to ask for a contact if I didn't work in PR.'

She inquired about presenter opportunities despite having no experience. Her candid nature and willingness to learn impressed the MTV team, leading to a screen test. Although she admitted to being naturally bad at presenting initially, MTV saw potential in her.

Learning to pivot

Despite DJing for high-profile names, including SZA and Doja Cat, and at events such as the Fenty Beauty launch in Australia, Flex found herself at a crossroads. She no longer felt aligned with the lifestyle and culture of DJing, which prompted her to re-evaluate her career path.

Flex's transition into influencing was not without its challenges. Despite her established reputation in niche, yet influential, circles, she had to start from scratch in a new industry, with around 5000 followers and with limited knowledge of the influencer landscape. However, her unique position at the intersection of DJing, beauty and influencing allowed her to carve out a distinct space for herself. 'I had a high level of influence in niche, but powerful, spaces. DJ scene — very niche. Girl DJ — very niche. Club DJ who's transferring into a beauty DJ — very niche. And so that gave me the opportunity to be the best at what I do.'

Listening to her mum

Early in her career, her mum gave her some advice: 'Stay in your lane'. According to Flex, 'It wasn't to suppress me or to encourage me to stop trying, but it was to stay focused on what I do best and stop looking to others for inspiration.'

Her journey into influencing, for instance, was marked by a conscious decision to diverge from the trends seen in traditional influencer posts, recognising that her value lay in offering something different. Her narrative underscores the significance of individuality or her 'individuality complex', as she calls it.

'My whole life, I've felt, like, a degree of grandiosity. I've always thought my ideas [were] interesting. I've always thought I've dressed really cool. I've always thought that I was not ahead of the game, but I carried a certain air of a secret sauce. I've always felt special. And working in this industry has really validated what I've already known. I'm like, yes, you're getting it. You see it.'

MAGIC BUCKET

Posting on social media

Flex emphasises the importance of authenticity and engagement over direct monetisation or brand partnerships. Her approach to sharing aspects of her daily life, such as journaling routines or other BTS activities, is not aimed at securing sponsorships from journal brands, for example, but rather at deepening her connection with her audience.

Flex opts for 'bids for connection', sharing interests and activities that invite engagement on a more positive and mutual basis, akin to extending a variety of threads for her audience to choose which ones to connect with.

Know yourself before you know the work

Flex Mami underscores the essential truth that individuality and self-awareness are pivotal to standing out in any field. 'And I think that you can read 1000 books about how to be the most proficient marketer, the most proficient philosopher, or whatever, but what makes you different from the next person is you. I'm talking [about] the way you speak, what you believe in, how you articulate ideas.'

She challenges the notion of mediocrity in exceptional personal brands, asserting there's no room for the ordinary. She argues that having a 'secret sauce' or a unique offering is non-negotiable for success. This belief is not about being the best in conventional terms but about having conviction in one's abilities and the uniqueness of one's approach.

'I'm not saying you need to be the smartest, the prettiest or whatever, but if you keep saying "there's nothing interesting about me" or "I'm really not good at this", then this is not the right place for you. You have to be good. You have to trust that you can deliver on what you're selling. You have to have conviction. And how you've expressed that will differ based on your personality. Not everyone can do that.'

PART V
What's next?

Now you've learned about the different stages of the marketing funnel, the secret sauce and the magic bucket, so what's next? It's time to bring it all together. But first some advice from Australian entrepreneur and business expert Mark Bouris.

CHAPTER 30

Advice from Mark Bouris: How to build a personal brand that spans decades

Mark Bouris AM is one of Australia's most high-profile entrepreneurs, with an extensive career as a business owner, financial advisor, CEO, media personality and mentor.

After selling his company Wizard Home Loans in 2004 for $500 million, Mark went on to become a chair of multiple boards and started Yellow Brick Road, where he is currently the executive chairman.

He is widely recognised for his TV appearances, including being the host of the hugely popular *The Apprentice* and *The Celebrity Apprentice* as well as *The Mentor*. He is the host of *The Mentor* podcast, which has over 2 million downloads and is consistently in the top five business podcasts in Australia.

Mark Bouris has established a successful career by building disruptive businesses, challenging the market and providing smarter solutions for consumers.

I originally wanted to interview Mark for his insights on personal branding, but as I spoke to him, I realised that he had so much more to give. His views on being a founder and public figure, being adaptable and social comparison, on top of building a personal brand and deeply understanding his audience, were incredibly insightful and valuable.

We spent hours dissecting the small business landscape and spoke about how founders can build a personal brand that captures and holds attention for the long term. These are Mark's six pieces of advice to grow your personal brand:

1. Understand and profile your audience

A founder or business does not just have one audience. Once you look closely, you will see that you have different groups of people with similar behaviours. For example, you may think that your target market is mums. However, when you go deeper, you may notice that you actually have three distinct audiences: young mums, mature first-time mums, and mums who are having their second or third child. You must analyse what they are searching for, why they are interested in you and your brand, and how to talk to them. Most of the time, they follow you because you were once in their shoes, or you currently are in their shoes.

You must have a deep understanding of your audiences, from their demographics to their interests and aspirations.

Mark is keenly attuned to exactly who is in his audience, and he has profiled them in detail, from the 18-year-olds to the retirees. He realised that there is one common denominator between each audience: they are all aspirational and driven. But he goes deeper than that:

> Let's talk about the teens that follow me. These kids usually go to a private school, but they aren't being picked up in a Rolls Royce. Their parents are working hard, and sometimes struggling to provide them with a good education. These kids respect their parents. These same kids don't get a gift from their parents to buy their first house—they have to borrow money. So, they do a lot of research on how to save a deposit and how to buy a property, and that's my territory. That's how they find me and follow me.

His intimate understanding of this audience allows him to provide the exact answers they are seeking.

Understanding why your audience shops with you or follows you as a business owner is the key to building your competitive advantage. You can own that space and that knowledge, and cement yourself as an authority.

Here are some actionable takeaways for understanding and profiling your audience:

- ◆ Craft personas for each segment of your audience, considering aspirations and life challenges.

- ◆ Understand the psychological and emotional drivers of your customer base beyond surface-level characteristics.

- ◆ Use your experience to provide tailored solutions to their problems.

2. Only speak to the people who like you

I don't care if there are people who don't like me. All I can do is talk about the things that matter to me to the people who like me. I can't control anything else. I don't try to convince anyone to like me.

When building a personal brand, you cannot appeal to everyone, and you shouldn't try to. The people most likely to resonate with you are the people with similar characteristics and values to you. Your experience and knowledge will benefit that group of people, and the focus should be on finding them and speaking directly to them.

According to Mark, it is almost impossible to convince those who don't agree with you to like you — it is a waste of time and energy. Rather than focus on trying to make those people happy, focus on the people who like you. That is a much better investment of your time because it builds a community of fans based on your actual values.

Here are some actionable takeaways for only speaking to people who like you:

◆ Write down who you want to target and make note of what they are interested in and why they would follow you.

◆ Write down who you don't want to target and make note of their characteristics and behaviours.

◆ When creating content and speaking to your audience, focus on benefiting the people who align with you. Try not to be too broad with your messaging as you risk losing the people who followed you based on your original ideas.

3. Trust is the key to staying relevant

Think about the people whom you trust most in your life. This could be your family or your closest friends. Why do you trust them? Even when you disagree or they say something hurtful, you still think of them as trustworthy. The reason for this is they are familiar, and you know what to expect from them. This familiarity and trust has been built over years. When you need help or if you have a question, these are the people you go to. They stay relevant in your life because you trust them.

Relevancy comes from trust. Trust comes from familiarity. Familiarity comes from time.

This is what Mark deems to be the key to his brand longevity:

> *People have seen me for a long time. My mindset and my vision remains the same, but I make small directional changes based on what's happening in the market and people follow me because they trust what I have to say. That level of trust has been built up over years and through multiple channels.*

Similar to building your business's brand trust with consumers, you need to be seen wherever your target audience is. Seeing your face in multiple locations over time builds familiarity and eventually trust.

A key takeaway is to leverage current topics (where everyone's attention is) to speak to your audience. Mark calls this 'currency' and gave an example of how he uses this currency to stay relevant:

> *Right now, one of the currencies is health and lifespan, so I decided to create something called Project 100, and every so often I will talk about it in my videos. I talk about how I want to live to 100, but I also talk about why. My 'why' is based around being an active grandfather and seeing my grandkids grow up. I need to use that currency and combine it with my love of health and*

fitness to stay relevant. I stick to my core beliefs but adapt to the current climate.

Here are some actionable takeaways for using trust to staying relevant:

◆ Start building familiarity by showing up consistently on multiple platforms.

◆ Use current news and trending topics in your industry and add your opinion to them. This creates relevancy in your personal brand.

◆ Don't try to build trust quickly. Trust is built and measured over time, so be consistent and have a long-term strategy.

4. Where attention goes, money flows

If you are not capturing attention and keeping it, you are not building a brand. At this time, attention is almost as important as money.

While Mark uses his knowledge of the economy, health and fitness, and finance to speak to his audience, he is very aware that he also needs to continue to surprise his audience and capture the attention of a new audience:

I always think about what will surprise my audience and get their attention quickly. Is it me lifting weights in a gym shirtless? Is it me getting into an ice bath and sitting in there for 20 minutes? What do I need to do in a physical sense that can get people's attention?

Richard Branson was a master of attention. Every so often, he would perform some kind of stunt — from dressing in drag to kite surfing with a naked model on his back. He did this because he knew it would capture the attention of his audience as well as publications around the world. He understood the power of doing things differently to stay interesting and in the forefront of people's minds.

Here are some actionable takeaways for where to put your attention:

♦ To capture people's attention, you need to think outside the box. Consistent content creation positions you as a thought leader, but surprising your audience occasionally will keep them engaged.

♦ Every so often think of a creative way to get people talking about you. This could include you travelling to another country to meet your audience, hosting an experiential event, dressing up as something funny for a cause, or even just holding up a big sign in a public place.

5. Stop comparing yourself to the 2 per cent

When I told Mark about the challenges I have had in my business and the mistakes that I've made, he said something that completely changed the way I was thinking:

When you think about your mistakes, you feel embarrassed and feel like you're not successful. But that's because you are thinking of the small percentage of people who are like you—hardworking, successful, doing a good thing, having a crack, taking risks—that's 2 per cent of people. The other 98 per cent of people don't take those sorts of risks. They have a job and have a low-risk, consistent-income way of life. If you take a step back and realise that you are in that 2 per cent, you'll feel good about yourself.

We all try to compare ourselves to the 2 per cent, but that's not where you should be looking. Those people are your peers, and they understand the risks and respect you for it. Those people don't give a shit about your mistakes. Instead, always look at the 98 per cent of people and understand how incredible it is that you did what they couldn't do. You are doing better than millions of people, remember that.

Here are some actionable takeaways to stop comparing yourself to others:

- Remember, only a small percentage of people dare to take the risks you're taking as an entrepreneur. Mistakes and recovery from those mistakes are a big part of your business journey and they set you apart from those who don't even start.

- Instead of comparing yourself to the very few at the top, recognise the courage it takes to be among the few who even try. This shift can change how you see your achievements.

- The people who understand and respect your journey are those who've faced similar risks. Their respect for you matters because they know the true value of what you're doing.

6. Be ready for any opportunity

Do not wait for opportunities to come to you. Start learning how to create opportunities and be prepared for them. Every day, Mark is prepared to go on television. He has multiple outfit changes in his office. He has even learnt how to do his own makeup for television. Everything is ready to go if he gets called by any TV network. In fact, he makes sure that he has been to the gym and is ready before the time that TV networks generally need an expert to talk about mortgages, finance or business. If the opportunity arises, he is prepared.

He also creates opportunities by partnering with a PR agent who has connections with executive producers on all the television networks.

When networks are looking to give a cheque or financial assistance to a business in need, they know they can call Mark as he is always ready to lend a hand.

Not only does he give back to the community, but he also gets exposure to a new audience:

> *What costs me $10000 in a cheque for a business owner who needs the money, also gets me awareness. Brands would need to pay over $500000 to get in front of a million engaged people.*

Saying 'yes' to opportunities that others may decline can result in unexpected positive outcomes.

If you are building a personal brand and want to speak at certain conferences, events or podcasts, figure out what their decision-making process is and what their audience craves. The producers of that event or podcast are always trying to find interesting and valuable speakers, and you need to position yourself as the best option. Get in front of the people organising the events and communicate your value.

Many opportunities come simply by asking for them or being ready when no one else is.

Here are some actionable takeaways for being ready for any opportunity:

◆ Create your own opportunities and be creative about it.

◆ Say 'yes' to opportunities, especially when you think others will say 'no'.

◆ If there are events or podcasts you want to speak at or on, find out what the organisers or producers are looking for, and position yourself as the best option. If needed, proactively approach those event organisers or podcast producers about speaking opportunities.

CHAPTER 31

How to build a community

Having a community is more powerful than any product you sell.

During the Black Friday sales last year, I went to a local shopping centre. As I walked past the Nike shop, there were two security guards standing outside and black rope cordoning off the entrance from the 50-metre line of people waiting to get their hands on Nike products at a 30 per cent discount. As I kept walking, I passed the Adidas shop. There were no security guards, no black rope and certainly no line of people. It was business as usual and the store wasn't very busy, even though they had a 50 per cent off sale.

It made me think about how two brands, extremely similar in their business model and products, can have such a vastly different customer demand. The most interesting thing about it was that it made me not want to enter the Adidas store — it just didn't feel exciting.

More than the products, the power of Nike lies in the community it has built. Nike's community-centric approach has created a powerful feedback loop. Community members are not passive consumers; they are active participants, providing valuable feedback, generating organic word-of-mouth promotion, and co-creating the brand's narrative. This engagement is priceless. It not only drives innovation and improvement in Nike's product lines, but also embeds the brand deeply into the lifestyle and identity of its community members. In essence, while Nike sells products, what it truly offers is membership in a community that embodies aspiration, achievement and a sense of belonging.

But, Nike is a big brand with lots of resources. The question is: can small businesses emulate the same community success with less money, fewer staff and less brand awareness? The answer is 'yes' — small businesses can not only learn a lot from big companies and implement those strategies in their own business, but the level of community engagement can actually be much higher. I am going to take you through the exact steps needed to build it from scratch.

The first important decision you will make when you start building a community is choosing who to exclude. This isn't about elitism or discrimination, it's about creating a space where a niche group of people feel connected through their opinions, values or behaviours. Allowing anyone and everyone into your community ultimately reduces the bond between members and their connection to your brand. On the other hand, the process of qualifying your audience attracts those who are really aligned with your brand or you as the founder.

Getting the first group of members right will ultimately define the future of your community, creating a space for them to not just learn about your brand, but also connect with each other. This could be through a Facebook group, an online community board or even a Slack channel. Remember, the ultimate goal of a community is not its size, but its ability to create brand ambassadors and lovers of your brand who speak about your brand and convince others to buy from you.

There are three key strategies to start and grow a brand community no matter how big your business is. If you nail these, you will create a cult-like following and an engaged audience:

1. make an enemy

2. BFF chit chat

3. charismatic leader.

There is one thing we need to talk about before diving into these strategies. In order to truly build a community, you must first build out your digital assets to broadcast and drive your community to your messages. Your digital assets are:

◆   an email database

◆   an app

◆   broadcast platforms: TikTok, a podcast, a newsletter

◆   relationship platforms: Instagram, a Facebook group, LinkedIn.

All communities start by having digital assets where you can talk to your audience. Without these, a community cannot be built. You do not need to have all of the digital assets mentioned, but you do need to have some of them. The reason I want you to have more than just one asset is because you are diversifying your communication, your sales and, most importantly, your risk. If one of these were to stop working, you can move your messaging easily without disrupting sales.

Let's get into the strategies:

1. Make an enemy

This is a concept that we covered in Chapter 10 about creating engaging content. The idea of 'making an enemy' also relates to creating a community because it uses emotion to connect a brand with its audience.

In 2021, Australia Post decided to change its pricing system for sending packages. If business owners wanted to send a package in their own packaging (and not Australia Post's packaging), even if it was the same weight and size, they were charged more for the delivery.

At Hero Packaging, we had hundreds of small business owners email us and tell us how upset they were that they had to start using plastic packaging again because Australia Post penalised them for using anything else, including our compostable packaging.

We made a decision to take a stand against Australia Post and their new pricing change. Our business values were to always support small business and to always support the planet so, as a small business ourselves, we took on the monumental task of fighting this change. We created content on all social platforms, we wrote emails to customers and we even reduced our pricing so we could help businesses use compostable packaging.

But the biggest thing we did was to start a petition on Change.org. Over the period of a month, we received over 31000 signatures and thousands of comments in support of our fight. Our community really backed us, and our social posts were shared and saved by thousands of people. This resulted in media publications featuring us, but also resulted in Australia Post reaching out and starting a conversation with us about what they can do better.

At every step, we kept our community in the loop, and they really felt like we were in this together.

Since then, we have received emails and social messages from our customers about how they will do anything to support us, even if that means their shipping bills are higher. This is all because we took a stand against an 'enemy'.

When you create an enemy and you stand up for what you believe in, you will start to build an audience of people who are like-minded and who will adore you. You have to be prepared that there will also be people who don't love you. That's really the point of making an enemy — you are finding your people.

It doesn't always have to be so serious. In 2012, Apple created a range of videos targeting the PC that showed two people: one representing an Apple computer and one representing the PC. The humorous ads used a young, cool and witty guy to represent Apple and an older, overweight and boring guy as the PC. It was Apple's representation of their 'enemy' that was an old and clunky PC. The ads were incredibly memorable and showcased Apple's benefits in an entertaining way by making fun of their enemy.

Now, an enemy doesn't need to be another business or a person. An enemy can also be a concept.

- Nike's enemy is the idea that greatness is only for elite athletes.

- Patagonia's enemy is the dirty denim trade.

- Fayt The Label's enemy is the idea that fashion is only for smaller-sized bodies.

As a small business, you need to identify your enemy. You need to write it down, print it out, stick it up somewhere. This is what you are fighting against. This is what your community is fighting against too.

But the idea here is to build a community, so simply having an enemy isn't enough. You need to talk about it and be loud about it. It should be one of your content pillars and you should aim to educate your audience about it.

Make sure that you create social content about it at least once per week and talk about it in email campaigns at least once a month.

Here are some tips on dealing with your 'enemy':

◆ Keep up-to-date with what is happening with your 'enemy'.

◆ Read news about the issue and keep educating yourself on it.

◆ See what's trending with your enemy on social media.

◆ Be at the forefront of education with it.

2. BFF chit chat

One of the biggest builders of community is when the audience feels like they know the business or founder personally. They form a parasocial relationship with the founder and speak about them and to them as a friend.

The term 'parasocial' was created in the early days of television where people watching shows would form a relationship with the actors on screen. Now, the term is used in a wider sense as people follow actors, influencers, athletes, musicians and businesspeople online. This parasocial relationship is an emotional connection between a prominent person and a fan. When this connection is to a founder of a business, it encourages people to engage with them and buy more things that they sell. They do this as part of their virtual 'friendship' and to feel close to them.

Go-To Skincare uses parasocial relationships exceptionally well. The brand's personality is based heavily on its founder, Zoë Foster Blake. Her wit shines brightly in Go-To Skincare's branding and content. Zoë also emphasises the parasocial relationship by personally replying to comments on the Go-To Skincare social channels. This makes their audience feel like they know her, or more importantly, like she knows them.

When you tag Go-To Skincare in your Instagram stories, they reply back quickly in a light-hearted and humorous way.

This style of community building is what I like to call 'BFF chit chat', where the audience believes that they are interacting with a friend, not just a business.

What I love about this method of building community is that it usually leads to something that all BFFs have: a group chat. This is a group forum where everyone in the community can talk about the brand and ask questions.

Let me tell you about one of the best brand group chats I've been part of: Mecca's Facebook group. In Chapter 24 we talked about the great loyalty program that Mecca runs, and how this expanded to Mecca Chit Chat, a Facebook group where their audience could talk about Mecca products, tell everyone about makeup hacks and ask each other for beauty advice.

The benefit of being in this group is that the members are the first to know about the newest products and they have access to masterclasses. But mainly, they can share their love and obsession for makeup and skincare with other like-minded people.

In October 2022, the Mecca Chit Chat group had 25000 people in it. As of October 2023, it had 144000. Think about that for a second. Currently, there are over 200000 people actively talking about or engaging with other people about a brand they all love.

Mecca has access to these people without having to pay for them through advertising. They have become brand advocates.

This is a very clever marketing strategy because whether your business has ten loyal fans or millions of them, you can create a platform for them to hang out and chat with each other and with you. For them to feel like they have exclusive access to you plays into the parasocial game and drives loyalty higher.

Tip

Creating a Facebook group for your brand is also a great way to send notifications to an engaged audience. When you have a sale or launch a new product, you most likely send an email and put a new banner up on the website. With a Facebook group, you can post the announcement and everyone in that group will see it as a notification. No spam filter. No unsubscribes. It's an incredibly powerful tool.

3. Charismatic leader

In September 2023, a new skincare brand called Paullie Skin launched. Within seven minutes, every product was sold out. This was done with no paid ads.

The reason for it selling out so fast was its founder, Anna Paul. Anna Paul is a social media influencer and content creator. She has a broad fan base of young men and women who relate to her for her candid, raw and every-girl persona. Her daily vlogs can see views in the millions.

Anna is the classic example of a charismatic leader. She has a die-hard following of girls, boys, women and men who will buy anything she creates or talks about. 'But she has 10 million followers', I hear you complain. 'Of course she will sell out of products.'

This misses the point and simultaneously makes my point. She gained those followers by being charismatic and speaking to her audience on their level. The product sales are just the icing on top.

See, being an engaging leader means that people are connected to you because of your personality. They want to learn more from you, and they truly enjoy seeing your content.

Whether you build that following up to 50 people or 10 million, like in Anna's case, you have that many people who are willing to buy whatever you sell. I want you to think about it this way — you have a product you want to sell. People are going to buy it because:

◆ it's a good product

◆ they love your brand

◆ they adore the face of the brand.

If you only focus on the product or the brand, you are missing out on targeting people who want to connect with another human. You're also forgetting that many brands will have a product similar to yours, so by focusing on product, it will come down to price to determine where they purchase from.

'But Anaita, I don't want to be the face of my brand. What can I do?'

You don't need to be the face of your brand, but you do need a face. The ideal situation is where the founder is the face because they are the ones with the purpose, the values, the mission, the story and they know the products intimately. But if you don't want to be the face, you can use someone else.

When someone sees a piece of content with the face of your brand, you want them to instantly recognise what brand it is. Over time, this builds trust, so when that brand replies to a comment or a DM, the audience believes it's the person doing it. That perceived relationship forms the foundation of a community.

What are the steps to becoming a charismatic leader?

The thing is, you already are a charismatic leader — people just haven't seen it. It's difficult to know where to start or what content to create to make your audience really adore you, but there is a framework you can use. Try these tips for social media content, email content, speaking content and even your 'About Us' section on your website.

TALK ABOUT PURPOSE

Your purpose is your secret sauce. It could be why you started this business. It could be why you wanted to stop working for someone else. It could be about your role models. It could be about what you want to change in the world. Whatever you are passionate about that is related to your business is the purpose I want you to talk about. You may already be talking about it, but I want you to 10x it. Talk about it more — say it louder.

KNOW YOUR CATEGORY INTIMATELY

There are two types of salespeople: those who can chew your ear off and talk and talk and talk and finally convince you because they're persistent, and those who know the product intimately and geek out over technical aspects of it and use it every day. In my opinion, the latter is the best type of salesperson. There is no question that stumps them. They don't talk fluff. They are knowledgeable and technical. That's who you need to be and who you need to showcase to your audience. By being the most knowledgeable person about a category or product, your audience will learn from you and trust your recommendations.

HAVE A PERSONALITY (WITH THREADS)

The thing I hate about having a conversation with someone is when I ask, 'How are you?' and they respond with 'Good'. It's then up to me to direct the conversation. They've given me nothing to ask about or dig deeper into. 'Good' is a terrible way to answer a question unless it's followed up with threads.

Threads means you give the person you're talking to conversational 'threads' so they can pick one of the threads and continue a conversation. For example, instead of saying 'Good', they may say, 'I've been good, but a little stressed about meeting a supplier on Monday. But luckily I'm flying to Fiji with the family on Tuesday so that will be fun.'

That's two threads. The conversation can now go down the path of the supplier or the trip to Fiji.

I want you to have threads online. Tell your audience a few things about yourself that will give them a connection point — something that they can relate to you with.

For example, my threads are that I:

- come from an immigrant family

- am a woman of colour in e-commerce

- am passionate and nerdy about digital marketing

- am a mum of three girls

- own and run a sustainable company

- love watching reality TV and true crime documentaries.

Tip

A big part of social media is being social. A mistake many business owners make is that they want everyone to watch their content, but don't feel like they need to engage back. This doesn't just mean replying to comments or DMs. I'm talking about taking an extra 15 seconds and sending a voice note back to them or even giving them a follow. Having that extra bit of social interaction is excellent for building positive brand sentiment. Engaging with your audience forges a connection that no competitor of yours is doing.

CHAPTER 32

Bringing it all together

You have successfully learnt all the strategies on how to get a consumer to turn into a customer and then turn that customer into a loyal fan.

But learning all those strategies is overwhelming without a structure, so I am going to show you how to structure your time so that you can work on those strategies consistently.

Before we dive into structure, I want to talk about how to measure the success of your strategies. As a business owner, you need to be looking at certain numbers/ratios frequently to see if the marketing strategies that you have put in place are actually working and growing your business. Without this, you are making uninformed decisions that could detrimentally affect your business.

Measuring marketing success

Many business owners look at metrics separately across different platforms, but that doesn't give you a holistic view of your business performance. Of course, each strategy has its own results to look at, but in order to see how they are all working as a whole, you should be looking at key business numbers that show you how your business is tracking.

There are eight numbers/ratios I want you to look at on a daily basis:

1. Revenue: Your total top-line revenue

2. Cost of goods sold: This is your landed cost of all products that have been sold

3. Profit: This is your revenue minus your cost of goods sold minus your expenses (this does not need to be 100 per cent accurate, but I'd like you to know a rough profit for the week)

4. Website visitors

5. Average order value

6. Number of orders

7. Marketing efficiency ratio: This is how much you spend on paid ads as a percentage of your revenue. It is calculated by adding all your paid ads costs and dividing that by your total revenue. A good marketing efficiency ratio sits between 15 and 35 per cent for most businesses.

8. Fixed costs per cent: This is the sum of all your fixed costs (including warehouse rent, staff costs, electricity etc.) divided by your revenue.

What I want you to do:

♦ document these numbers in a spreadsheet

♦ every tab is a new month and within each tab, you create a table that has each day of that month on the top row, with the first column having each of the numbers/ratios listed above

♦ look at these numbers and ratios on a daily/weekly/monthly basis so you can see the fluctuations and trends based on what you implement.

How to structure your weeks

Learning about marketing strategies to grow your business is exciting, but overwhelming when your to-do list is already pages long.

This book hasn't been designed to make you implement all the strategies at once. It is a comprehensive list of everything your business needs to grow and can be woven into your marketing plan.

If you don't already have a marketing plan in place for each week, then this is where I want you to start. Giving your to-do list some kind of structure will help you feel more organised and get more done. This is what I want you to do:

- ◆ To create this plan, either use a planning tool (Trello, Click Up or Notion are a few of my favourites) or a spreadsheet. You don't need anything fancy, just something that you can easily access and refer to throughout the week.

- ◆ Use a weekly calendar view or create a table with the days of the week as the headings. We are going to use this to write a list of tasks that you will do every day for the coming week.

- ◆ First, fill in the mandatory tasks on each day; for example, packing orders, customer service, paying bills and team meetings. Mark these are in bold, and, if you want, you can allocate a time next to them.

- ◆ Next, add in content creation as a priority task every day. Mark this is in italics.

- ◆ Finally, fit in one to two marketing strategies from each stage of the funnel (refer back to the MOFU, TOFU, BOFU sections for a refresher).

- ◆ Create a weekly plan for the next four weeks and ensure that you are covering off most of the strategies that we have spoken about in this book.

Your weekly plan

I have created an example plan below for four weeks' worth of business and marketing tasks. Remember, **bold** = mandatory tasks; *italics* = content creation.

WEEK 1

Monday	Tuesday	Wednesday	Thursday	Friday
Check last week's numbers	Team meeting	Accounting meeting	Do the pay run	Team meeting
Customer service (replying to emails)	Customer service (replying to emails)	Customer service (replying to emails)	Customer service (replying to emails)	Customer service (replying to emails)
Pack orders	Pack orders	Pack orders	Pack orders	Pack orders
Create content	*Create content*	*Create content*	*Create content*	*Create content*
Update Meta ads	Write blog posts	Send emails	Improve a customer touchpoint	Work on community-building strategies

WEEK 2

Monday	Tuesday	Wednesday	Thursday	Friday
Check last week's numbers	**Team meeting**	**Accounting meeting**	**Do the pay run**	**Team meeting**
Customer service	**Customer service**	**Customer service**	**Customer service**	**Customer service**
Pack orders	**Pack orders**	**Pack orders**	**Pack orders**	**Pack orders**
Create content	*Create content*	*Create content*	*Create content*	*Create content*
Send emails	Contact five to ten influencers about a new product launch	Check and update Google Ads	Improve three product or service listings on your website and make them engaging and SEO-friendly	Review Meta campaigns and make changes to spend and ad creatives

WEEK 3

Monday	Tuesday	Wednesday	Thursday	Friday
Check last week's numbers	**Team meeting**	**Accounting meeting**	**Do the pay run**	**Team meeting**
Customer service	**Customer service**	**Customer service**	**Customer service**	**Customer service**
Pack orders	**Pack orders**	**Pack orders**	**Pack orders**	**Pack orders**
Create content	*Create content*	*Create content*	*Create content*	*Create content*
Make a list of content ideas	Create a TikTok ad to get new followers	Improve another customer touchpoint	Send emails	Check Meta ads

WEEK 4

Monday	Tuesday	Wednesday	Thursday	Friday
Check last week's numbers	**Team meeting**	**Accounting meeting**	**Do the pay run**	**Team meeting**
Customer service	**Customer service**	**Customer service**	**Customer service**	**Customer service**
Pack orders	**Pack orders**	**Pack orders**	**Pack orders**	**Pack orders**
Create content	*Create content*	*Create content*	*Create content*	*Create content*
Review your returns policy to see how you can make it better	Write blog posts	Send email campaign	Check Meta ads	Write a press release about your business and upload it to Linkby or send it journalists

At the start of every month, I want you to make a plan similar to this. It's incredible how much you can get done when you write out what you want to achieve.

The final recap

There is no magic wand or fairy dust when it comes to growing your business. It all comes down to understanding where your target market is and targeting them with the right strategies to push them further down the funnel until they become customers and, eventually, loyal fans. That's what this book has aimed to teach you.

In this moment, it is possible for business owners to sell anything online; you just need to understand and follow the marketing funnel.

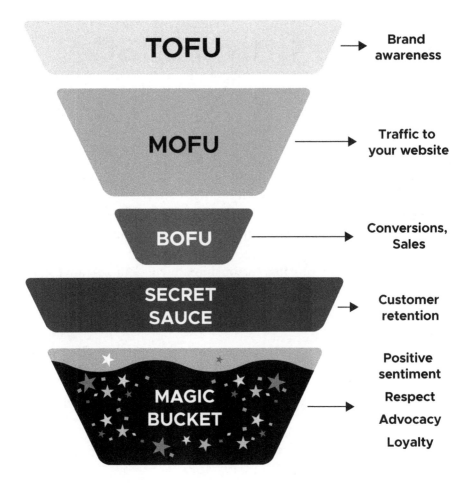

Top of FUnnel (TOFU)

Aim for boosting your brand awareness by identifying where your target market is online and showing up through multiple channels, remembering that a consumer must see your brand over a dozen times before they have any sort of familiarity with it.

Leverage strategies such as Meta ads, TikTok, influencers and PR to get in front of a new qualified audience, also known as a 'cold audience'.

Middle of FUnnel (MOFU)

The goal of the MOFU is to leverage brand familiarity and trust and get consumers to visit your website. The consumers in this section are 'warm' because they have heard about you and like you enough to have engaged with you on social media, but haven't added your products to their cart.

Use strategies such as SEO, Google Ads, Meta ads, emails and Instagram to persuade them to browse your website.

Bottom of FUnnel (BOFU)

This audience, also known as a 'hot audience', is extremely close to purchasing from your store. They just need a small amount of persuasion to get them over the line. As business owners, our first instinct is to offer them a discount to turn them into customers, but there are other strategies you can try, such as email flows, Meta ads, and website optimisation. These are the most effective ways to convert this audience.

Secret sauce

You have already turned a consumer into a customer, and now you want to start building a relationship with them and encourage them to return to your store.

Retaining a customer starts with an incredible customer experience. It's important to focus on delivering an exceptional experience rather than simply a product or service. Email marketing strategies are the best way to communicate with your customers and grow their retention.

Magic bucket

Having loyal and raving fans is the ultimate goal of any business. Your goal is to turn your repeat customers into brand advocates (your magic bucket) — people who adore your brand and talk about it to their friends and will choose you over your competitors every time.

In order to achieve this, you need to use community building strategies, develop a personal brand and treat your customers as VIPs in your email marketing.

No matter how many people are in your magic bucket, they need to feel like they are in an exclusive group.

My last piece of advice

About six months ago, I was talking to my mum about how I was anxious that I wasn't doing enough to grow Hero Packaging. I was complaining that my sales weren't as high as I wanted and that I was tired all the time. Her words in that moment completely shifted how I was feeling and changed my perspective on business:

Why don't you try and enjoy your business? Find happiness in the things you do instead of looking too far ahead. You have a beautiful business with customers who really like you. Enjoy it.

It was simple, but it blew my mind. I had forgotten the joy of being in business — I was caught up in implementing every marketing strategy, comparing myself to other businesses, and feeling anxious about my future prospects. I had forgotten my driving forces.

I had forgotten that when my children's school calls me because one of them is unwell, I can pack up immediately and pick them up. I don't have to ask anyone for permission.

I had forgotten that I have the privilege of working from anywhere and taking breaks whenever I want.

I had forgotten that creating content was about building a wonderful community and not about getting more likes.

I had forgotten that I left a corporate job because I felt like a tiny cog in a huge machine, and I got yelled at in front of dozens of people for a small mistake.

I had forgotten my driving forces.

Since that conversation with my mum, I have changed the way I approach my work. I printed out those driving forces and stuck them on my laptop and I focus on finding happiness in the everyday tasks that I am doing.

Of course, I want you to implement all the strategies in this book and scale your business, but above all else, I want you to be excited about the process.

Remember why you started and enjoy your business.